D0881106

FIVE
COUNTERREVOLUTIONISTS
IN HIGHER EDUCATION

Five Counterrevolutionists In Higher Education

IRVING BABBITT
ALBERT JAY NOCK
ABRAHAM FLEXNER
ROBERT MAYNARD HUTCHINS
ALEXANDER MEIKLEJOHN

By Michael R. Harris

Foreword by W. H. Cowley

Corvallis:

OREGON STATE UNIVERSITY PRESS

TO

Scholar, Teacher, and Friend

FOREWORD

COLLEGES AND UNIVERSITIES have evolved from man's efforts to comprehend and to control his environment and himself. Over the long stretches of prehistory and history these efforts begat the medicine man and shamans of primitive peoples, the magi and priests of early civilizations, the sophists and philosophers of the Greek city-states. In all eras such men have been the guardians and critics of the knowledge and values of their societies and also the teachers of promising youths. When they formed associations the precursors of present-day colleges and universities emerged.

Historians and educationists often characterize the antecedents of today's higher educational institutions as aristocratic; but in the sense that most people understand aristocracy, the judgment has little validity. Not until the nineteenth century did the colleges and universities of the world—Oxford and Cambridge partially excepted—begin to be seriously concerned with the interests of the socioeconomic aristocracies. Instead, they served their limited conceptions of the intellectual aristocracy even though during some periods their chief patrons, many of their teachers, and most of their students came from the wealthy classes. Thus not until the relatively recent past did colleges and universities come to be recognized by the great establishments of society and by people in general as not only important, but indeed, as vital to the welfare and progress of men and nations.

Today the ivory-tower image of the campus has all but disappeared both among academics and generally. Consider these commonplace facts: (1) all European countries, Russia in the forefront, are spending substantial fractions of their budgets to vitalize the educational and research activities of their existing universities, to build new ones, and to finance increasing numbers of students; (2) African and Asian peoples are following their example avidly and are sending legions of their brightest youths abroad for advanced study; (3) more than 7,000,000 young Americans are currently attending higher educational institutions compared with about 50,000 a century ago; (4) the federal government and the fifty states are pouring larger and larger sums into advanced study and research, while government helmsmen orate endlessly about their imperative importance; and (5) captains of industry, the great majority of whom are alumni in sharp contrast with their predecessors, vie with editors in seconding these pronouncements.

Clearly colleges and universities have become pivotal societal agencies serving mounting waves of youths of both sexes and from all social classes. In turn, most other institutions have come to depend upon them for their trained manpower, for their frontier knowledge-power, and for some precious kinds of moral-power. In short, they have ceased being sequestered retreats from the world's hurly-burly and have been transformed into its paramount powerhouses.

As might be expected, these dramatic changes have not been approved by some academics. The value systems of the most vocal of such critics have their roots in ancient Greece whose philosophers typically denigrated all varieties of practical education. These mentors held that earning one's living interferes with good citizenship and personal cultivation, that making and selling the products that led to Hellenic prosperity required only low-level intelligence, and hence that apprentice-trained slaves and metics freed the intellectual elite for Higher **Things.**

In *The Republic,* for example, Plato assigned mechanics and farmers to the lowest order of his utopia, and he recommended that unruly soldiers be disciplined by demoting them to it. Aristotle agreed with him. Both of them approved of athletics, politics, and war which they did not consider to be work. Farming, technical crafts, and commerce, however, they deplored as both banausic and brutalizing. Their point of view, shared by their aristocratic contemporaries, remained strong in the West until the recent past; and it still dominates many Oriental, African, and Hispano-American societies as well as the thinking of American academic breast-beaters such as those assessed in this book.

Mr. Harris, like the present writer, considers his five subjects to be in some degree backward-looking romantics; but he has sought to understand and to explain them rather than to emphasize the negative results of their romanticism. He has asked me to write this foreword, I take it, because he agrees with a passage included in the syllabus of one of the courses he took with me beginning about a decade ago. It reads: "Some people see more, feel more, know more than 'practical men' believe possible. Their purposes and projects appear to be romantic and usually are, but a few of them turn out to be right. Right or wrong, however, they bestir people—the young in particular—to thoughts and actions which, challenging vested interests or breaking new ground, give each age its tone and flavor."

W. H. COWLEY
Palo Alto, California 1969

CONTENTS

PREFACE

During the latter part of the nineteenth century, American higher education underwent a revolution which changed its basic purposes: It became operationally useful to society. Prior to that time, the American college had not concerned itself with the kind of general education necessary to prepare its students for a direct understanding of their environment. It had likewise shunned professional education and faculty research of immediate value to society. American colleges basically remained isolated from the mainstream of American life. From roughly 1870 to 1900 all this changed. New universities emerged and old colleges transformed themselves in order to serve society in an operationally useful manner. A virtual revolution had occurred. The goals, the personnel, the structuring—in fact, virtually the whole system—of American higher education were radically different after 1900 than a third of a century earlier.

The notion of operational utility lay behind all the major phases of this revolution. As used in the following pages, this term specifically denotes the policies of colleges and universities which are intended to develop the ability of students to play useful roles in society and which will result in the production and communication of useful knowledge.

During the latter part of the nineteenth century, three developments arose relating to operational utility. In the first place, institutions of higher learning made shifts in their internal educational policies by broadening their concept of general education to include a study of knowledge useful for understanding the contemporary world. In conjunction with this they brought in new programs concerned with research and vocational preparation. Research did not always relate to the operational needs of society, but it generally did. In the second place, besides these on-campus changes, colleges and universities developed new educational programs for people beyond the campus proper. Extension became an important part of many universities, and it usually reflected the demands by the nonacademic community for operationally useful knowledge. In the third place, professors increasingly left the classroom to give advice to men of affairs. These three nineteenth-century developments are the complementary themes of operational utility, and they drastically altered the whole shape of American higher education.

American colleges and universities experienced a revolution in their whole make-up when control of them shifted during this period from the hands of the adherents of nonutilitarian education to the advocates of educational operational utility. Chapter One relates in some detail the precise nature of this revolution. It presents background material about the historical relationships between higher education and the operational needs of society, traces in broad outline the transformation of American colleges and universities, develops the concept of operational utility, and gives in the University of Wisconsin an outstanding example of one of the new universities of operational utility.

By the turn of the century, the traditions and rationale of higher education for operational utility had taken firm root in American education. They had even affected the policies of the traditionally classics-oriented ivy league colleges. At that time it might have appeared foolish or quixotic to challenge the validity of this development, but critics nevertheless did challenge it. They wanted colleges and universities to drop their concern with the operational problems of society.

Because they opposed the nineteenth-century revolution in higher education, these critics were educational counterrevolutionists. In a very real sense they wanted to undo the pattern of higher education in the twentieth century which had been formed during the late nineteenth century. Their challenge to the status quo forms an important part of the intellectual history of higher education and, indeed, of the intellectual history of twentieth-century America itself. The body of this book explores in depth the ideas of five leading counterrevolutionists, primarily those ideas expressed in their writings and speeches in the six-decade period from 1900 to 1960.

These critics of twentieth century higher education opposed the new general and professional education; they disliked research of operational utility; and they believed education through extension services wrong. Professorial consultations with men of affairs also was bad for higher education, they believed. Each of the five represents a different approach to the criticisms of operational utility, and for the most part their rationale for opposing education of operational utility do not agree with one another. Their solutions likewise differ. Thus they offer good opportunities for examining the bases of modern higher education from several critical positions. Chapter Two summarizes the general approach of each of the five, and Chapters Three through Seven deal with each critic's views specifically.

I first became interested in this subject while studying with Professor W. H. Cowley, and I wish to thank him for invaluable aid at numerous levels of my development. His stimulating teaching, criticism, and concern stand as models for me. This book itself arose from a suggestion made by David M. Potter, and I appreciate his rigorous criticism of it in an earlier stage. To my graduate adviser, Professor Otis A. Pease, I owe a special debt for his open-minded, progressive approach to life and learning. With his assistance, I have been able to follow my interests, a pleasure not always possible under today's academic routine.

Alexander Meiklejohn and Robert Maynard Hutchins graciously granted me interviews, and I trust I have not betrayed their kindness with unjust words. I also wish to thank Henry S. Kariel for his criticism of Chapter Three, Robert M. Crunden for his of Chapter Four, and Bancroft Greene for his of Chapter Seven. Michael Polioudakis worked well with me as a research assistant, and Ruth Mather and Naomi Harnagel typed all sorts of unrequired pages for me. I am grateful to them.

To my mother and father go special thanks for providing the benefits which come of good parents. Their assistance has meant a great deal.

MICHAEL R. HARRIS
Claremont, California, 1969

FIVE
COUNTERREVOLUTIONISTS
IN HIGHER EDUCATION

CHAPTER ONE

The Ideal and Practice of Higher
Education for Operational Utility

---

*"Higher learning" of the modern world . . . has grown
and shifted in point of content, aims and methods in response to the changes in habits of life that have passed
over the Western peoples during the period of its growth
and ascendancy.*

THORSTEIN VEBLEN, 1918

IN A POLITICAL DICTATORSHIP, higher education
exists to perpetuate the established order. The rulers use
education at all levels to reinforce their control over society,
and they use educational institutions as a means of indoctrinating the youth to accept their beliefs and practices. The ruling
elite may well allow freedom of thought and teaching in areas
which do not relate to its values such as some areas of science,
for these tend to serve as a means of increasing the technical
means of social control at the disposal of the government. Yet,
any idea which touches upon political values is directed toward
enhancing the position of the rulers.

In the United States, higher education also exists to
perpetuate the established order. A crucial difference exists
between the purpose of higher education in this country,
however, and that in a dictatorship. In the United States, at
least in theory, the people themselves, not a small ruling elite,
determine the basic political direction of the nation. The

established order in American democracy consists not of a well defined political and social hierarchy; it consists of somewhat fluid, changing groups of people. Under the Constitution, regulated change has become a central part of American ideology. America is conservative in its adherence to traditional political forms, but it is liberal in the access which people of different social backgrounds have to its positions of power. Higher education in the country as a whole thus exists to serve no special interest group or point of view.

Higher education should preserve, discover, and transmit knowledge which the people think important. No social, economic, or political elite should dictate to the entire country which type of higher education American youth is to receive. If representative democracy is to work, the people must receive any information they wish and make their own choices about the policies their government is to institute for them. As institutions concerned with knowledge, colleges and universities become central agencies for assisting people to achieve the goals they want.

The American people, however, have not arrived at a consensus about the good life, other than a rather vague commitment to the freedom of the individual; and no agreement exists about the nature of this freedom. A notion that the good life rests upon material abundance has gained wide acceptance, but confusion abounds regarding the use of that abundance other than its partial direction toward the creation of more material abundance. Most Americans would like man's intellectual and spiritual potential to develop, but as a body politic they have not defined intellectual and spiritual goals.

This lack of consensus becomes particularly evident when the interests of the various constituencies of colleges and universities make themselves clear. Students, for example, enter college without a uniform set of goals. Some go to college for vocational training; others to get away from their parents; or to participate in organized athletics; or for the simple intellectual challenge of college study. The interests of employers, faculty, parents, religious leaders, and sports enthusiasts add complexity to the purposes behind the current practices of American colleges and universities.

Because of the curious composition of American society, American higher education as a whole has not catered to the wishes of any one group. In a sense, such a thing as American society does not exist. Instead of one monolithic societal organization, America consists of diverse groups through which power is diffused. Politically, this pluralism manifests itself in a federal system with three independent branches of government on the central level and a fragmentation of power through the fifty state governments and numerous local governments. Economically, American pluralism expresses itself in the various forms of competitive and countervailing organizations which wield economic power. Religiously, the vast array of independent denominations overwhelms foreigners. The hundreds of thousands of other voluntary associations like fraternal lodges, women's clubs, professional bodies, and ethnic societies provide other centers for the life of the American people. This decentralized social power has provided the basis for diversity of control in higher education.

The designation of higher education into the two sectors, public and private, fails to recognize the great variety in American educational control. In the majority of foreign countries, a central government controls all universities. In the United States, final control of the major tax-supported colleges and universities rests with each of the fifty state governments. Futhermore, some cities control colleges and universities. The federal government directly controls only a handful of colleges and universities, such as the military academies and some special graduate institutes. Churches, with real differences between them, control hundreds of colleges and universities; and a large percentage of colleges and universities, especially many of the distinguished ones, remain directly responsible to no organization other than their own boards of trustees.

With more than 2,400 institutions of higher learning in the country competing for students and money, American higher education has been forced to remain responsive to the wishes of the groups beyond the campus which can support them. A college or university must, for instance, cater to the interests of students for knowledge, prestige, and fun, or the students will go elsewhere. In order to cultivate outside support, American colleges and universities have entered into close relationships with various political, religious, and economic groups wielding power. Like any major organization, a college or university acquires a certain momentum of its own independent of outside influence, but in the long run colleges and universities have developed to serve outside constituencies by providing the men and the knowledge which the complex called American society has asked for.

Throughout the revolution in higher education during the late nineteenth century, American colleges and universities attempted to shape their educational programs to the needs of society. General education in the undergraduate years now assists a student to understand how the world about him functions; vocational courses provide entry into an earning field. In the minds of many, no worse epithet than "irrelevancy" can be hurled at a course. University extension attempts to take the university directly to the people and deal with problems of interest to them. Even a great part of research conducted by universities relates to the immediate needs of society.

Many professors spend a good part of their time in direct service to society. Scholarship demands high competence in a delimited field of inquiry, and when socioeconomic problems fall within a scholar's area of study, his knowledge should enable him to render expert advice. Abreast of the latest developments in his specialty, the competent scholar is acquainted with viewpoints other than those readily evident to the layman. Hence the academic man can often serve a role of great usefulness to governmental and industrial organizations in need of expertise. Since the need for experts is great in American society, professors in practical disciplines supply a welcome reserve of the specialized knowledge which American society requires.[1]

BACKGROUND

The Medieval University

Universities and society have traditionally had a close relationship to each other.[2] Universities in their present form can trace their origins to the Middle Ages, and medieval universities were institutions of operational utility. In fact, they were primarily professional schools. The University of Salerno arose in the eleventh century as a medical school. The greatest university of Southern Europe, Bologna, emerged in the twelfth

[1]For discussions of the problems involved in professorial participation in politics see: Walter Lippmann, "The Scholar in a Troubled World," *The Atlantic Monthly*, CL (1932), 148-152; Robert K. Merton, "Role of the Intellectual in Public Bureaucracy," *Social Forces*, XXIII (1945), 405-415; Roberto Michels, "Intellectuals," in *The Encyclopedia of the Social Sciences* (New York), VII, 118-126; Merle Curti, ed., *American Scholarship in the Twentieth Century* (Cambridge, 1953), pp. 17 ff.; Richard Hofstadter, *Anti-intellectualism in American Life* (New York, 1963), pp. 197 ff.; and Seymour Martin Lipset, *Political Man* (Garden City, 1963), pp. 332 ff.

[2]In the following treatment of the general history of higher education, I have relied heavily on W. H. Cowley's "Overview of American Colleges and Universities" (Mimeographed copy, Stanford University, 1960). See also Hastings Rashdall, *The Universities of Europe in the Middle Ages,* (Oxford, 1936); Stephen d'Irsay, *Histoire des universités francaises et etrangeres des origines a nos jours* (Paris, 1933-1935); Frederick Rudolph, *The American College and University* (New York, 1962); and Laurence R. Veysey, *The Emergence of The American University* (Chicago, 1965). For a different approach to revolution in American higher education, see the brilliant study by Christopher Jencks and David Riesman, *The Academic Revolution* (Garden City, 1968).

century as a school of civil law.   Paris, the pattern for universities in Northern Europe, trained theologians and scholars for the Church.   Doctors, lawyers, and theologians all held very practical positions in the society of the Middle Ages, and the universities existed to train these leaders.

Although some of what the modern age understands as general education was included in the medieval university, practical subjects designed to enable students to make their way in the world of affairs dominated the universities.   Even the conceptual work carried on by the faculty related rather explicitly to questions which the medieval mind considered of immediate relevance.   In fact, the leading English authority on medieval universities has claimed that the academic disciplines of the Middle Ages were too practical.   The universities of the Middle Ages failed to cultivate in the least what the twentieth century understands as culture.[3]

Universities flourished as long as they supplied graduates skilled in the professions needed by society.   The proliferation of universities during the fourteenth and fifteenth centuries came because of the increasing demand for highly trained lawyers and administrators.   Universities languished only when they turned their attention to studies unrelated to the immediate operational needs of their environment.   During the sixteenth, seventeenth, and eighteenth centuries, they gave more attention to literary subjects of interest primarily to young gentlemen of leisure, and the university movement lost much of its vitality and strength. Many great thinkers of the age found institutional homes in academies outside the universities rather than within them.[4]

---

[3]Rashdall, *Universities*, III, 456.

[4]Martha Ornstein, *The Role of Scientific Societies in the Seventeenth Century* (Chicago, 1938), pp. 257 ff.; T. H. Huxley, *Science and Education* (New York, 1894), pp. 102 ff.

The Nineteenth-Century German University

Universities did not again assume an important role in the immediate life of any nation until Germany found itself prostrate during the Napoleonic Wars. In the winter of 1807-1808 the philosopher Johann Gottlieb Fichte delivered fourteen lectures entitled *Addresses to the German Nation*. In them he called for a rejuvenation of the moral, intellectual, physical, and vocational potential of the German people through education. With the opening of the University of Berlin in 1810, he began to see his plans realized, and German universities came to play a crucial part in the rehabilitation of Germany.

Dedicated to national service, German universities immersed their students in the latest scientific and social knowledge. Their graduates were qualified to staff the higher echelons of the German political and industrial bureaucracies. In order to provide students with the latest knowledge, German universities required that every professor not only teach but also carry on research. Impregnated with the ideals of rationalistic science which came to characterize all studies, German scholarship thus contributed vast sums to the storehouse of both theoretical and practical knowledge. Students equipped with this knowledge contributed to the military and industrial power which enabled Germany to force itself into the councils of the world's leading powers by the end of the nineteenth century.

The German ideals of research and national service proved mutually beneficial, for as the nation prospered its scholarship surpassed that of any other country. Germans, however, did not force their scholars to study the immediate operational problems facing the nation. They recognized that the pursuit of knowledge for its own sake would eventually result in practical benefits to Germany, and they therefore allowed scholars broad freedoms to explore the unknown. National service did not imply the direct solution of practical matters. It meant the creation of new knowledge and the education of students to understand it. The immediate contribution of German universities to society lay in the production of a large group of men educated in the latest theories and indoctrinated to serve the state.

The quality of German academic life attracted students from around the world, including the United States. Between 1810 and 1915 approximately 10,000 Americans crossed the Atlantic to study in German universities. When they left Germany, many carried with them the ideals of research and national service. During the early nineteenth century, men like George Bancroft, Joseph Cogswell, Edward Everett, and George Ticknor returned home and called for the reform of American higher education along the lines of German academic life.

The Nineteenth-Century American Literary College

In early nineteenth-century America, no university as such existed. The American literary college characterized American higher education before the Civil War. It did not relate to the operational needs of society. It was able to supply neither the personnel nor the knowledge needed to solve the operational problems of a dynamic industrial country. Instead of relating closely to its environment, it held to one over-riding purpose: the disciplining of the student's mind. While doing this, those in charge of collegiate policy expected they would also produce Christian gentlemen with a common educational experience.

The concept of a disciplined mind stemmed from the Greek philosophers. They had maintained that the mind consists of faculties such as attention, discrimination, judgment, memory, thought, and will. According to their theory, these faculties could be developed by exercise just as appropriate physical exercise develops the muscles of the body. Educated Americans of that time believed the college existed primarily to give this kind of mental exercise to the students.

They built the curriculum, therefore, around subjects they believed to be of disciplinary value. Students devoted approximately two-thirds of their time to the classical languages. The colleges taught science, but it was not experimental. Students read about it in books. A course in moral philosophy or Christianity and mathematics on the level of arithmetic, geometry, or algebra made up the rest of the curriculum.

The colleges prescribed these studies for everyone. No matter what students were to do later in life, the college attempted to give all students the same education so that they would share a common intellectual heritage.

The men controlling the early-nineteenth-century American colleges failed to realize the radical nature of the future. They neither foresaw the rapid changes in the world of ideas nor imagined the dramatic shift from an agrarian and rural society to one characterized by industrialism and urbanism. The age of science and technology which was about to burst forth lay hidden from their view. In their desire to stay upon safe, trodden paths, they isolated the college from the currents of change flowing about it.

They attempted to hold the college to the traditions characteristic of the leisure class since the days of Plato and Aristotle. They adhered to the ideals of the influential "Report on the Course of Liberal Education" of Yale College, written in 1828 largely under the aegis of President Jeremiah Day and a professor of classics, James L. Kingsley. Under the spirit of this document, the American college reaffirmed the worth of the classics for mental discipline and rejected practical subjects and research.

TRANSFORMATION OF AMERICAN HIGHER EDUCATION

For some time men had been working to direct the energies of American higher education toward solving society's operational problems. In 1749 Benjamin Franklin had written

Proposals Relating to the Education of Youth in Pennsylvania.
He had wanted the new Academy and College of Philadelphia
to educate manual, clerical, and professional workers. Later,
during the early nineteenth century, Thomas Jefferson outlined
a program for the University of Virginia which allowed the
student a choice between seven prescribed courses of study, some
of which related closely to the contemporary scene. He was
interested in allowing students to study subjects with practical
implications if they wished. Neither of these proposals, however,
had much effect upon American colleges and universities.

During the nineteenth century, college enrollment began
to decline, as did the percentage of students attending
institutions of higher learning. Too many people did not see
any meaningful relation between classical education and what
they wanted to do in life.

Aware of this, Eliphalet Nott, president of Union College
from 1804 to 1866, instituted the first science and engineering
courses in a traditional American college in 1828. His colleague
at Brown, Francis Wayland, president between 1827 and 1855,
wrote an approving book in 1842 entitled *Thoughts on the
Present Collegiate System in the United States.* He said that
American colleges and universities must provide education for
merchants, mechanics, and industrialists or face extinction.

A few other educators also held the same opinions. They
were not concerned with research, but they did want instruction
in technology available in the United States. The Rensselaer
Polytechnic Institute, established in 1826, attempted to become
operationally useful by preparing teachers to apply experimental
scientific knowledge to agriculture and industry. In 1834,
beginning with Delaware and Vermont, some states also tried
to relate higher education to their operational problems by
founding agricultural colleges. Furthermore, even some literary
colleges admitted that something should be done by allowing
scientific schools to be built near them. In 1847 Harvard

established the Lawrence Scientific School and Yale initiated the Sheffield Scientific School. Dartmouth followed in 1867 with the Thayer School.

The hold of the classicists upon higher education did not loosen, however, until the German university ideal began to be accepted in America. Although Henry Tappan, president of the University of Michigan from 1852 to 1863, had tried to establish a German-style university, only the election of Charles W. Eliot to the presidency of Harvard in 1869 eliminated the classicists' domination.

Eliot, who remained in office until 1909, virtually revolutionized the old literary curriculum. First of all he strengthened the professional schools. He brought them under closer supervision of the university administration, required at least high school graduation for admission to them, and broadened their curricula. For example, he immediately required a high school diploma for admission to the medical school and lengthened its course of study from nine to twenty-seven months. Secondly, he extended the elective system in the 1880's. He allowed the undergraduates to study whatever they wished, including subjects of operational utility, after certain basic requirements had been satisfied. Finally, he established a graduate school of arts and sciences above the undergraduate college. Professional training, election, and graduate work in the arts and sciences all shifted Harvard's emphasis from subjects of no operational utility to those of possible utility.

Essentially Eliot was attempting to improve the educational character of the American college by broadening the curriculum rather than destroying it. He realized that higher education had to be of some practical significance to society if it were to flourish.

Although Eliot did much to change the nature of the old classical college, his contemporary, Daniel Coit Gilman, the dynamic president of Johns Hopkins University, possibly did much more. Although implementing graduate programs into

Harvard's curriculum, Eliot had not favored the acceptance of research as a legitimate function of a university. Gilman, on the other hand, thought that it was of utmost importance.

When Johns Hopkins opened its doors in 1876, Gilman had committed it to graduate instruction and research. Gilman thought that American universities should primarily be research centers and only secondarily teaching institutions. He failed to exclude all undergraduate instruction from the university, but he fully initiated research into an American university, and American higher education as a whole moved into an era when research became as important a path to academic distinction as undergraduate teaching.

During the last half of the nineteenth century, another force crucial in moving American colleges and universities from their classical orientation also had been developing. The land-grant college movement, championed by men like Horace Greeley, an influential New York politician and newspaperman, and Jonathan Baldwin Turner, a leading Illinois educator, had been gaining momentum. In 1862 Abraham Lincoln signed the Land-Grant College Act. It gave federal lands to the states to sell for the endowment of colleges teaching agricultural and mechanical arts as well as other scientific and classical subjects. It thus gave formal recognition to the position that colleges and universities should be institutions of direct operational utility to society. Since state legislatures provided the funds for the state colleges and universities established under the Land-Grant College Act, the measure further ensured that the new institutions would remain close to the wishes of the people.

THE CONCEPT OF OPERATIONAL UTILITY

Behind these late-nineteenth-century changes in colleges and universities lay the concept of higher education for operational utility. This concept implies that the *raison d'être* of a college or university consists in serving the immediate needs of society. Put in the briefest terms, higher education for operational utility is the education to equip a student to operate in society at large or to perform the specific tasks demanded by his job. In such an education, a person acquires the knowledge and techniques necessary for modern society to function. He seeks to understand his physical and social environment so he can control it. Thus a future politician, or for that matter any voter, can learn the manner in which political parties operate. A future physician can acquire the knowledge and skills to practice medicine. The ideal of operational utility for higher education, however, not only concerns the training of students. It also entails the production and communication by colleges and universities of the specific, detailed information needed for nonacademic men to perform their roles effectively. Thus colleges and universities become the source of both the trained manpower and the knowledge to keep the wheels of society rolling.

The impact of the concept of higher education for operational utility changed the basic pattern of American higher education. The nineteenth-century literary college had devoted itself almost entirely to a prescribed general education which bore no direct relationship to the problems of American society. In the new colleges and universities the nature of general education itself changed and two new basic varieties of education entered: that concerned with vocational technique and that concerned with the expansion of the boundaries of man's basic knowledge.

Under the new and still current notion of general education, almost any imaginable subject can be studied. A professor and some students simply have to desire to examine it. Interestingly enough, too, most of the new courses of general education relate to the operational needs of society. Thorstein Veblen perceived the basic operational orientation of the elective system when he stated:

It was in the introduction of electives, and presently of alternatives and highly flexible curricula, that the move first set in which carried the American college off its footing as a school of probation and introduction to the scholarly life, and has left it a job-lot of ostensibly conclusive short-cuts into the trades and professions.[5]

Veblen misunderstood the function of the early American college, for it primarily produced gentlemen and men of affairs, not scholars. He also failed to see that the elective principle is not simply a vehicle for vocationalism. In the first place, a student can elect a program similar to the old classical curriculum. He might attempt to build his character and choose courses which he might think important for that objective. In the second place, elective courses can relate to the operational needs of society in a nonvocational fashion. Disciplines without necessarily vocational overtones like psychology, economics, political science, and history focus to some extent on problems of immediate social importance.

Gone for the most part is the preoccupation of the old American literary college with character. Society has other objectives for higher education to attain. It wants as many people as possible informed about immediate problems. At the end of the nineteenth century, character training remained important in the eyes of many educators, but it lost its place as the *raison d'être* of American higher education.

Besides the new variety of general education, the entrance of vocational education into the curriculum fits directly into the concept of higher education for operational utility. Vocational courses equip a student with knowledge and skills of very direct utility. The classical colleges served operational ends to the extent that they enabled the student to acquire the

---

[5]Thorstein Veblen, *The Higher Learning in America* (New York, 1957), p. 209.

general knowledge and social skills expected of a minister, lawyer, or other professional man, but they did not teach the specific techniques necessary for the practice of the profession. Under the new educational ideal, both professors and students devote a great deal of energy to topics of interest primarily because of their vocational value.

This direct response to the vocational needs of society was novel to American higher education and during the latter part of the nineteenth century threatened to overshadow all general education. Colleges and universities were coming to emphasize subjects of a practical nature such as agriculture, business, engineering, and home economics. Many students were using their freedom of election to find a niche in the industrial or governmental world. They were more interested in getting a good position than in becoming Christian gentlemen.

Research also came into prominence in the new colleges and universities, and it also related to operational utility. Much of it applied to matters of public and private concern. Operational concerns with cattle breeding, human illness, and industrial management all fell within the purview of the new university professors. Admittedly, research which ignored practical benefits also entered higher education, but applied research has come to receive the greatest acclaim, and research of no utility in many respects is justified to the public upon the basis of eventual service to society. As Clark Kerr has recently said:

> . . . *the university is being called upon to produce knowledge as never before—for civic and regional purposes, for national purposes, and even for no purpose at all beyond the realization that most knowledge eventually comes to serve mankind.*[6]

The shift from a basically literary education in the old American college to the modern curriculum heavily scientific

---

[6]Clark Kerr, *The Uses of the University* (Cambridge, 1963), p. vi.

and technological in nature reflects society's recognition of the practical worth of science and technology. The classics, with their basically subjective approach to reality, have yielded to science, with its basically objective approach. Science, useful in the material world, might eventually aid the practical American in mastering his physical environment. Subjective studies, on the other hand, do not appear to have immediate material value.

These changes in the university's program together with the introduction of extension services were the most significant nineteenth-century marks of the concept of operational utility upon higher education. Through extension universities began to offer many courses resembling those given on their own campuses. Not all courses were of operational utility but many were. Subjects ranging from law and accounting to agriculture and mechanics were listed in the catalog along with Hebrew and Greek. If the university could assist society to operate better by training its own students in these areas, it supposedly could increase its utility to society by training as many people as possible through extension. If more people could gain the knowledge necessary to operate efficiently in their jobs or on the general sociopolitical scene, society itself would be better equipped to solve its operational problems.

Much the same rationale lay behind the last phase of higher education for operational utility: professorial consulting with men of affairs. If academic men possessed knowledge useful to groups within society, they should communicate it to men of affairs so the knowledge could become operative. When government needed experts to solve public problems, it should call upon professors for advice. Industrial firms in search of better operating procedures also might consult with members of the business, economics, engineering, or similar departments. Medical practitioners could receive advice from professors in medical schools. Farmers could ask for detailed information from authorities in agriculture departments. In fact, almost any group in American society might turn to someone on the faculty of a university when it needed an intelligent opinion regarding its interests.

The curricular changes, extension services, and professorial consultations reflect the impact which the ideal of operational utility made upon American higher education. Let us see how these changes affected one particular university, one that several historians of American education have called the outstanding example of a university relating to immediate societal needs.[7]

OPERATIONAL UTILITY AT THE UNIVERSITY OF WISCONSIN

The University of Wisconsin shortly after the turn of the century provides a good model of an American university of operational utility to society. It was not atypical of American universities of the day. It simply developed the broadest program of practically oriented extension courses in the country, and its professors rendered unparalleled service to state government.[8]

The Curriculum

The curriculum of the University of Wisconsin did not differ greatly from those of other major universities, and it clearly reflected the desire for a close bond between the University and its environment. It had law and medical schools for training lawyers and doctors. In a primarily agricultural state, its Agricultural College was strong. Its College of Letters and Sciences reflected a strong vocational orientation. It taught not only nonprofessional courses in the humanities and sciences

---

[7]Lawrence A. Cremin, *The Transformation of the School* (New York, 1961), pp. 87, 161 ff.; Hofstadter, *Anti-intellectualism*, pp. 197 ff.; Rudolph, *American College and University*, p. 363; Rush Welter, *Popular Education and Democratic Thought in America* (New York, 1962), p. 258.

[8]For an extended history of the University of Wisconsin, see Merle Curti and Vernon Carstensen, *The University of Wisconsin* (Madison, 1949). Chapter Three, II, 87-122, and Chapter Seventeen, II, 549-594, are especially relevant.

but also pharmacy, journalism, and teacher education. Civil, chemical, mining, and mechanical engineering rounded out the curriculum.

Courses of direct operational utility by no means absorbed the energies of the teaching staff. Anglo-Saxon, Aramaic, Assyrian, Gothic, Greek, Hebrew, Latin, and Sanskrit along with Arabic, Bulgarian, German, French, Italian, Portuguese, Russian, Spanish, and significantly enough in a state with a large Scandinavian population, all the modern and ancient Scandinavian languages comprised the language offerings of the University in 1910. Other basically nonvocational disciplines had similar breadth. The University fitted into the dominant educational pattern of the day by permitting its undergraduate and graduate students to study virtually anything they wished.

The people of the state strongly supported this curriculum, for they wanted the University to train personnel who could deal with the needs of society. Granting admission to any high school graduate, the University was attempting to prepare students to function on the contemporary economic, political, and social scene. The University of Wisconsin drew national attention because of its close connection with the state.[9]

University Extension

The men responsible for shaping university policy believed that a state university should work with the general public through direct means. It should not only prepare its regular students for citizenship and jobs, but it should also influence all citizens to support good government and to improve their

---

[9]For contemporary discussions of these tendencies see, for instance, E. A. Ross, "The Middle West: State Universities and Their Influence," *Century*, LXXXIII (1912), pp. 874-880; Charles Richard Van Hise, "Educational Tendencies in State Universities," *Educational Review*, XXXIV (1907), pp. 504-520; Charles Richard Van Hise, "The University and the State, Commencement Address at the University of Wisconsin, June 22, 1910," *La Follette's Weekly Magazine*, July 2, 1910, p. 7; and Lincoln Steffens, "The Mind of a State," *La Follette's Weekly Magazine*, Jan. 9, 1909, pp. 5, 13.

vocational skills. By elevating the level of the public's under-standing of operative knowledge, the university could thus contribute to the creation of a better society.

The task of converting the entire population of the state of Wisconsin into students of the University became the goal of university extension. Charles R. Van Hise, who became president of the University in 1903, argued that no agency for cultivating the ideals and abilities of the people surpassed university extension. It could educate the general public to appreciate methods of analytical thinking and thus put complex social problems into a rational perspective. With this perspective, solutions to complex problems would come more quickly than by trial and error.[10]

Although university extension had long been important in the University's program, under President Van Hise extension courses of great operational utility took their place beside subjects characteristic of the nineteenth-century literary college. The University offered courses in areas as diverse as potato growing and classical literature. The teaching of classical subjects simply extended the traditional function of the American literary college to a broader population, but farmers' institutes, homemakers' conferences, and other special institutes gave the people an opportunity to use the extension program as a means of finding solutions to operational problems.

Agencies such as the Bureau of General Welfare provided answers to thousands of questions regarding agriculture, economics, education, engineering, government, manufacturing, sanitation, and sociology. University shops and laboratories supplied information about building materials, commercial fertilizers, fuels, ores, and soils. The Municipal Reference Bureau published data on subjects such as paving, playgrounds,

---

[10]Edward A. Birge, in *Memorial Service in Honor of Charles Richard Van Hise* (Madison, 1919), p. 21; Charles McCarthy, *The Wisconsin Idea* (New York, 1912), p. 125; Frederick Jackson Turner, *The Frontier in American History* (New York, 1948), p. 285.

sewage disposal, and social centers. The Bureau of Debating and Public Questions sponsored open discussions on matters of current interest such as capital punishment, the commission form of government, direct election of senators, immigration, the initiative, the referendum, trusts, and women's suffrage. At one time it also sponsored a national conference on civic- and social-center development. Across the state, extension stimulated the discussion of vital public issues.[11]

Expert Advice

In addition to the use of university extension in educating the public, some professors advocated technical assistance by the University staff to provide factual information to public bodies. They wanted University graduate students and seminars to investigate agriculture, labor, utilities, railroads, and taxation. The School of Economics, Political Science, and History should, they urged, study affairs of government and suggest solutions to questions of labor and capital. President Van Hise wholeheartedly approved of these professorial proposals. He emphasized that the state had the right to demand advice from the University in all technical areas. He liked the idea of the University becoming the scientific and technical adviser to the commonwealth.

One of the most progressive political leaders in American history, Robert M. La Follette, who became governor in 1901, agreed with Van Hise. An alumnus of the University, he saw it as a source of the specialized knowledge he needed. Thus by 1910 forty-six professors were serving the state. Most of them furnished technical services by advising the commissions established under the progressive reformers who ruled from 1901 to 1914. They served on the Conservation Commission, Dairy and Food Commission, Fish Commission, Geological and

---

[11]Ross, "The Middle West: State Universities and Their Influence," pp. 874 ff.

Natural History Survey, Library Commission, Poultry Association Board, Seed Inspection Board, State Live Stock Sanitary Board, and other technical bodies.[12]

As technical cooperation became common, a broader sort of advising developed, namely, consultation on basic policy between La Follette and certain members of the University. This feature of higher education in Wisconsin was not typical of the national movement toward operational utility in colleges and universities, for no other university in the country developed anything like it in scope. In Wisconsin several professors of economics and political science actually drafted legislation affecting the civil service, electoral procedure, labor conditions, railroad regulations, and taxation. Furthermore three of them served on commissions established by the legislation they had written.

This feature of higher education for operational utility points out that the new developments did not force colleges and universities to deal only with procedures and to neglect values. The services of faculty members on technical commissions may have served to reinforce the basic structure of society, but the consultations with the governor and legislators did not necessarily do so. In creating new fundamental policies, the professors in Wisconsin were challenging the status quo. Classroom and extension courses likewise dealt with policy as well as technical questions. Thus higher education for operational utility was not simply a means of perpetuating and extending established patterns of action.

In Wisconsin, as elsewhere, the new pattern of operational utility in higher education did not grow because of a commitment to it as an abstract idea. It became dominant because the need for it was felt by the people supporting the

---

[12]Howard J. McMurray, "Some Influences of the University of Wisconsin on the State Government of Wisconsin" (Unpublished doctoral dissertation, University of Wisconsin, 1940), p. 15.

University. Wisconsin progressives realized that the problems of a new age required new uses of higher education. The people had to come into touch with the appropriate knowledge. Common sense would no longer suffice. John R. Commons, a University of Wisconsin economist, asserted, "A fool can put on his coat better than a wise man can do it for him," but maintained the state would be better off if wise men rather than fools were in control.[13] If the uneducated could not cope with the complicated demands of an industrial society, colleges and universities had to educate the people to solve the technical and policy problems facing the state. In early-twentieth-century Wisconsin, the people turned to their university for assistance with their operational problems. Since the University was willing to help the state, the University became operationally useful.

According to the theory behind higher education for operational utility, both society and the university would benefit from university involvement in the nonacademic world. For instance, one Wisconsin professor, Balthasar H. Meyer, maintained that cooperation between professors and men of affairs would keep the former in touch with life and keep their studies vital.[14] Believing that a professor and his students should acquire practical experience, his colleague Commons stated, "Academic teaching . . . is merely brains without experience. . . . The practical extreme is experience without brains. One is half-baked philosophy—the other is rule of thumb."[15] A professor qualified to gain practical experience should do so in order to "be able to prove his theories by the

---

[13]Quoted in Turner, *Frontier in American History,* p. 286.

[14]Balthasar H. Meyer, "Discussion of Doctor Paxson's Paper," American Historical Association, *Report,* I (1907), 122.

[15]John R. Commons, *Myself* (New York, 1934), p. 160; Richard T. Ely, *Ground Under Our Feet* (New York, 1938), p. 186.

hard facts of actual events."[16]   Through active participation in the life of society, professors could remain sensitive to the real needs of society.

Advocates of universities for operational utility maintained that the United States possessed no better institutions than universities for realizing its ideals.   University teaching would produce graduates capable of immediately assuming responsibility in society; university extension would aid all the people to better themselves; and university research would give society a broader choice of techniques in dealing with new social, economic, and political problems. Furthermore, the consultation of scholars with governmental and industrial groups would help them cope with a complex technological age.   Thus proponents of higher education for operational utility declared that university teaching, extension, research, and consulting would benefit both the university and society.

---

[16]McCarthy, *Wisconsin Idea*, p. 189.

CHAPTER TWO

Critics of the New Ideal

This era of great expansion, of changing goals, and of almost rootless flexibility would of course breed its own mistakes, its own disappointments, even a counter-revolution of sorts.

FREDERICK RUDOLPH, 1962

THE CHURCH AND THE UNIVERSITY are probably the two most traditional social organizations in Western civilization, and thus the shift of American higher education to the practices of operational utility naturally brought criticism. Many observers believed strongly in the basic values of the American literary college. They feared that higher education for operational utility spelled the demise of higher learning in America, and they raised a multitude of objections in attempts to reverse the dominant new trend. Probably every established college or university in the country which adopted any phase of the new educational ideal did so in the face of considerable criticism, and this criticism did not die after the new patterns became entrenched.

The ideas of five men in particular expressed the views of the major American writers who were critical of higher education for operational utility: Irving Babbitt, Albert Jay Nock, Abraham Flexner, Robert Maynard Hutchins, and Alexander Meiklejohn. Their names appear extensively throughout the literature of higher education, and they received more publicity than others because of their critiques of American higher education. They attracted extensive and serious attention from respected intellectual and educational leaders. Numerous other critics obviously existed, for debate characterizes academic life. The others, however, generally followed the arguments advanced by these five.

Irving Babbitt (1865-1933) thought that American colleges and universities should sponsor research to discover new humanistic standards of culture and then inculcate these standards in an elite student body. He did not want higher education to concern itself with operational problems of society. He maintained that the popular, democratic impulses of the country needed the discipline and control which an elite dedicated to high cultural standards could provide. Thus he stressed the importance of the proper kind of research and teaching in colleges and universities and lamented the failure of educational leaders to follow his advice. According to him, they were neglecting the most vital cultural standards required for civilization in favor of education of operational utility. Preeminent among a group of thinkers called the New Humanists, Babbitt played a prominent role in the intellectual ferment of the 1920's. Because of his influence upon important writers like T. S. Eliot, George R. Elliott, Norman Foerster, Paul Elmer More, and Robert Schafer, he commanded considerable respect among intellectuals.

Albert Jay Nock, (1870-1945) criticized higher education as Babbitt did. He too concerned himself primarily with cultural standards. His position differed from Babbitt's in that he did not advocate research to find new cultural standards. He held that the only purpose of colleges and universities lay in the formation of character in students. Basically an educational reactionary, he strongly recommended a return to the principles of the early-nineteenth-century literary college. They alone could develop character. Perhaps because of his strong individualism, he did not lead any school. Even as editor of perhaps the nation's most prestigious literary magazine of the early 1920's, *The Freeman*, he did not cultivate a distinguished group of disciples. A friend of H. L. Mencken, he voiced the same caustic disdain of American democracy as the editor of the *American Mercury*, but he deserves attention because of the unique and striking nature of his ideas.

Abraham Flexner (1866-1959) became a controversial national critic of operational utility in education with the publication of his 1930 book, *Universities, American, English, German*. If not the most renowned twentieth-century attack upon the notion of operational utility in higher education, it stands among the leaders. In sharp contrast to Babbitt and Nock, Flexner opposed the notion that colleges and universities should focus upon cultural standards and the building of character. He would not have objected to Babbitt's recommendation for discovering cultural standards, but he would have rejected character-building as a function of American higher education. Believing that the discovery of any new conceptual knowledge would result in the progress of civilization, he wanted the university to concentrate its resources upon research. Concern with matters unrelated to it would hamper the quest for truth. He feared that concern with short-range operational problems was diverting talent from the pure research which in the long run would bring the greatest return to society. He received money to establish his ideal educational institution, and the Institute for Advanced Study at Princeton came into being. Although some question the general educational significance of the Institute, it nevertheless occupies a distinguished position in the ranks of academic institutions.

Robert Maynard Hutchins (1899-   ) and Alexander Meiklejohn (1872-1964) adhered to educational theories which to some degree resulted in the same practices. They both favored a general educational program based upon great books which was to strengthen democratic tendencies in America. Hutchins favored an ideal of higher education centered about abstract, rational, metaphysical principles. He opposed higher education for operational utility because he believed that it diverted attention from the greatest contribution a university could make: the establishing of those principles needed as a basis for the proper ordering of society. Meiklejohn, on the other hand, wanted higher education to develop social intelligence in students. Defining this as the ability to control one's social environment, he differed with the advocates of operational utility primarily because he believed that they concentrated on immediate technical problems. He thought that control comes through a philosophical understanding of the broader ideological issues facing a society.

Other major educational thinkers such as Mortimer Adler, Stringfellow Barr, Scott Buchanan, and Mark Van Doren in many respects resemble either Hutchins or Meiklejohn. In practice all have cooperated, most notably in the Great Books of the Western World program and the Saint John's College innovations.

Babbitt, Nock, Flexner, Hutchins, and Meiklejohn belong together for one reason, namely, their common opposition to the concept of operational utility for American higher education. Each held a different view of the nature of the student entering colleges and universities, each in a different way hoped for the creation of a society unlike the society he confronted in twentieth century America, and each proposed a different educational program to attain his goals for man and society.

They did not agree with one another in the social and political reasoning behind their educational positions. Babbitt and Nock both rejected the idea of a powerful state, and they called for an education to develop strong individuals capable of operating in a society free of governmental restrictions. Flexner took no explicit political stance in his writings. Hutchins and Meiklejohn, on the other hand, assumed that the individual can only develop within a democratic, collectivist political society, and they wanted students to be prepared to exercise their responsibilities in it.

Their ideas led them all to oppose the dominant practices of American colleges and universities. Operational utility in their opinions endangered the particular educational and social ideals in which each of them respectively believed. Like the advocates of operational utility, all of them thought that colleges and universities should relate to the needs of society. They were critics because they all thought that the proponents of operational utility, in focusing upon immediate operational problems, neglected the more fundamental, long-term needs of society.

Each of them believed in his day that civilization itself was dying and that higher education should act as a revitalizing force. All of them except Flexner wanted a revolution in human affairs to parallel that which had been made in the material world. Fear at the passing of an old culture and a certain despair at the slow arrival of a new one characterized the thought of all of them. A relativism devoid of standards appeared to be sweeping away the vestiges of traditional Western civilization, and they warned that education for operational utility diverted attention from the real problems of culture. Higher education for operational utility to them was merely training followers to execute skillfully the policies of others instead of developing leaders who could create new ideas and values for society.

All of them therefore shared a strong dislike for the concept of operational utility. Contemporary patterns of elective curricula, extension programs, and widespread professorial consultations did not meet their respective goals for higher education.

CHAPTER THREE

IRVING BABBITT:
Civilized Standards and Humanistic Education

To repudiate the traditional Christian and classical checks and at the same time fail to work out some new and more vital control upon impulse and temperament is to be guilty of high treason to civilization.

IRVING BABBITT, 1932

PREEMINENT AMONG THE NEW HUMANISTS, Irving Babbitt opposed educational innovations made in the name of operational utility. He denounced the notion that universities should function in response to immediate societal needs.[1] He did not want institutions of higher learning to provide advice to men of affairs, initiate extension programs, or adjust their internal educational programs toward matters of operational utility. He wanted universities to discover cultural standards and colleges to inculcate them. Thus he opposed any phase of undergraduate education or faculty research which did not relate to the humanistic standards he proposed.

---

[1]Norman Foerster, at one time a student of Babbitt's, actually wrote more about higher education than Babbitt, but the outline of his ideas is contained in Babbitt's writings, and his thoughts follow naturally from Babbitt's assertions. Likewise, although other New Humanists like James Luther Adams, Seward Collins, George R. Elliott, William F. Giese, Frederick Manchester, Frank J. Mather, Paul Elmer More, Gorham Munson, and Odell Shepard differed from Babbitt in some respects, in general they followed his ideas.

Although born and raised in Ohio, Babbitt spent virtually all his professional life at Harvard as a professor in the French Department.[2] During his years there he wrestled with one central problem: the development of the cultural standards which could lead twentieth-century man, stripped of his faith in traditional Christianity, to a balanced, happy life. He himself had begun life with a firm belief in Calvinism but had lost it. He kept his faith in certain tenets contained in Calvinism, but he believed they needed a new form. He thought that the rest of society was losing its values and that it needed new formulations of the truths embodied in the older traditions. He believed that education could help supply the new forms needed for living the good life, and he devoted his own professional life to the search for them.

Babbitt led a scholarly life, spending his career within the confines of his classrooms and his office in Harvard's Widener Library. He published widely, and his students carried his message across the land into the lecture halls of universities and onto the pages of literary magazines. One of his acknowledged followers, for instance, Norman Foerster, initiated reforms as director of the School of Letters at the University of Iowa in accord with Babbitt's basic assumptions. As Babbitt's former students gained prestige, they drew attention to him and his teachings. They brought interest in his ideas to a climax in 1930 with the publication of a collection of their essays, *Humanism and America.*[3]

The book brought a flurry of comment, capped by C. Hartley Grattan's 1930 book, *The Critique of Humanism.*[4] During the 1920's, earlier critics of Babbitt had included an odd variety of people. Some of Babbitt's friends thought that

---

[2]Frederick Manchester and Odell Shepard, eds., *Irving Babbitt; Man and Teacher* (New York, 1941) , pp. ix ff. In this memorial written by Babbitt's friends and associates, his wife has written a good biographical sketch.

[3]Norman Foerster, ed., *Humanism and America* (New York, 1930) .

[4]C. Hartley Grattan, ed., *The Critique of Humanism* (New York, 1930) .

Sinclair Lewis had used the word Babbitt in his 1922 book of the same name purely to spite him. H. L. Mencken in 1924 had vilified Babbitt as the personification of the sterile Puritanism which Mencken believed plagued America. T. S. Eliot had acknowledged Babbitt as perhaps his greatest teacher but differed with him when Babbitt refused to insist upon a supernatural basis for humanism. In 1928 Howard Mumford Jones offered bitter criticism that was soon outmatched by the reviews of *Humanism and America*. Walter Lippmann, in a short, vitriolic article in the *Saturday Review*, labeled Babbitt and New Humanism as pure dogma and nothing more. Only a Communist named V. F. Calverton outdid him: the *New Masses* printed Calverton's article entitled "Humanism: Literary Fascism," which characterized Babbitt as a lackey of the capitalist classes. Edmund Wilson's accusation of Puritanism seemed mild in comparison.[5]

The deepening of the depression turned men's attention from the New Humanists, but the movement did not die. Even today intellectual figures such as Nathan Pusey, the president of Harvard, and Russell Kirk, the literary and political writer, acknowledge the central influence Babbitt exercised upon them. In 1960 Harvard posthumously honored Babbitt with the endowment of the Irving Babbitt Professorship of Comparative Literature.

Interestingly enough, Babbitt did not approve of the Harvard of his day. He entered Harvard as a student in 1885

---

[5]H. L. Mencken, "The State of the Country," *American Mercury*, III (1924), 123-125; T. S. Eliot, "The Humanism of Irving Babbitt," *Forum*, LXXX (1938), 37-44; Howard Mumford Jones, "Professor Babbitt Cross-Examined," *New Republic*, March 21, 1928, pp. 158-160; Walter Lippmann, "Humanism as Dogma," *Saturday Review of Literature*, March 15, 1930, pp. 817-819; V. F. Calverton, "Humanism: Literary Fascism," *New Masses*, V (1930), 9-10; Edmund Wilson, "Notes on Babbitt and More," *New Republic*, March 19, 1930, pp. 115-120. See the analysis of this criticism by Seward Collins, a leading New Humanist, in "Criticism in America," *Bookman*, LXXI (1930), 241-256, 353-364, 400-415; LXXII (1930-1931), 145-164, 209-228.

and joined the faculty in 1894. Thus he knew well the new university ideals initiated by Charles W. Eliot, and he detested them. The free elective system, in his opinion, was destroying the humanistic education which he believed necessary for regenerating society, and the scientific approach which characterized even literary research did not relate to the creation of new cultural values. He felt the University was neglecting the central question of cultural and individual standards in its efforts to be of operational utility to society. Thus it was failing on two counts: it was not educating its own students so they would develop proper values; and in attempting to serve society, the university was not helping society to establish social goals corresponding to the needs of man's basic nature.

Essentially then, Babbitt was not objecting to a university's being of social significance. He was condemning current university practices because he thought they were concerned with the mechanics of running a technical society rather than with the cultural values necessary for shaping mankind's destiny. His criticism of the idea and practice of higher education for operational utility rested upon this distinction between the ends of society and the means to attain them.

THE STANDARDS OF NEW HUMANISM

Babbitt believed that a university should exist for the sole purpose of discovering personal and cultural standards and passing them on to its students. Hence an understanding of his humanist standards is necessary in order to understand his position on higher education.

Élan Vital and Frein Vital

At the basis of Babbitt's thought lay two concepts: the *élan vital* and the *frein vital*. More psychological than sociological in nature, these concepts resembled the tenets of his Calvinist forefathers who had believed in a struggle within each individual between God's spirit and man's natural carnality.

Babbitt's *élan vital,* a concept which he consciously adopted from Henri Bergson, is similar to the Calvinist notion of the unregenerate man. It refers to the impulse or the subrational intuition supposedly within each man which lusts after knowledge, sensation, and power. This urge knows no limit and impels every man to expand his dominion without end. Conditioned by this concept, so widespread in Protestant America, Babbitt thought that the *élan vital* would impel men to clash in their unlimited drives for domination.

Just as Calvinist theology had also perceived a spirit of light within certain men, Babbitt saw a force operating in opposition to the *élan vital.* Babbitt's *frein vital* stood for an inner control which can check the power of the *élan vital.* While Calvinism considered this control a gift of God, Babbitt believed that men acquire it from their civilization.

Rejecting all theological formulations for his belief, Babbitt asserted the existence of the *élan vital* and the *frein vital* as immediate facts of consciousness obvious to any perceptive observer. He realized the similarity of his dualistic view of man to the Pauline doctrine of the spiritual and depraved man and believed that Christians might accept his views on religious grounds. He himself, however, thought that the humanistic bases of classical higher education provided sufficient premises.[6]

As Babbitt looked at the world of affairs, he interpreted everything in terms of his concepts of the *élan vital* and *frein vital.* The struggle between the two constituted the battle between good and evil, and they constantly opposed each other within each man individually and all mankind collectively. Since these forces made up the inner life of every man, no one could escape this conflict. Since every society was ruled by men in whom either the *élan vital* or *frein vital* was dominant, no

---

[6]Irving Babbitt, *On Being Creative* (Boston and New York, 1932), p. 261; Irving Babbitt, *Spanish Character and Other Essays* (Boston and New York, 1940), p. 243.

society could escape acting in the manner characteristic of the dominant *vital*.

He thought that the triumph of the *frein vital* brought men cooperation, peace, and happiness. On the other hand, when the *élan vital* had broken the check which the *frein vital* had imposed upon it, the strong would seek domination over the weak, and conflict would break out. Contemplating World War I, which he saw as the result of an uncontrolled *élan vital*, he feared that the *élan vital* would consistently overwhelm the *frein vital*.[7]

Babbitt thought that the American literary college had disciplined the student and helped to check the *élan vital* by strengthening the *frein vital*. Therefore he believed that the destruction of the old curriculum had removed a powerful cultural force working for peace in the world. He argued that higher education for operational utility was neglecting the undergraduate education necessary to strengthen the *frein vital* which alone could peacefully check man's natural impulse to destroy his higher self and conquer his neighbor.

The research of universities also failed to relate to the real problems posed by contemporary civilization. Babbitt maintained that the *frein vital* should not smother the expansive desire of the *élan vital*, but rather channel it in a right direction. The problems of what constituted a right direction, however, required careful investigation, for since the demise of traditional Christianity among thinking men, Western civilization had arrived at no new consensus of values. The university should be searching for those values.

In developing this line of thought, Babbitt did not oppose a tie between the needs of contemporary society and the programs of American colleges and universities. He simply maintained that the problem of establishing proper cultural standards for society overshadowed all other possible educational

---

[7]Babbitt, *Spanish Character*, pp. 213-214.

concerns. His advocacy of the study of man's subjective life contrasted sharply with the ideal of operational utility, which tended to focus upon science and the world of affairs.

If men are to attain peace and avoid conflict, they indeed have to devise a means of establishing standards by which they can live. If careful observers such as university professors would give the attention to the study of human nature which they have to physical nature, they might be able to work out cultural patterns which would enable men to live dynamic and progressive, but peaceful, lives. Babbitt correctly saw the need for attention to the values sorely needed by Western civilization. Man should expand his control over himself as he extends his control over nature.

The Establishment of Standards

Babbitt worked out a system for university professors to use in approaching the problems of cultural standards. He first distinguished man's imagination from his reason and his will. These categories resembled the faculties of the brain which were used as a rationalization for the curriculum of the classical college, but he did not intend to defend the old system. He conceded that faculty psychology was outdated. He realized that all divisions of men into powers or faculties were more or less arbitrary, but he felt them inevitable, if only as instruments of thought. In them he saw the expression of "certain obscure and profound facts of experience."[8] Through the correct use of them, Babbitt claimed, men could arrive at standards.

Imagination can reach out and seize likenesses and analogies. Although Babbitt never mentioned his contemporary, Carl G. Jung, his doctrine of the imagination paralleled Jung's idea of the collective subconscious. Both held that a man can transcend his own time and place and arrive at concepts totally

---

[8]Irving Babbitt, *Rousseau and Romanticism* (New York, 1960), p. 137.

unlearned through his own environment. The virtually magical powers of the imagination enable it to grasp matters common to the entire human race. The highest use of the imagination permits one "to grasp the abiding human element through all the change in which it is implicated."[9]

Babbitt thought that without the use of reason, however, the imagination would function in the realm of fantasy instead of in reality. He urged the use of analytical reason to test the activity of the imagination by reference to the actual data of experience.[10]

He believed strongly that by examining all possible historical and contemporary human experience, university professors and others could find a huge array of facts about human nature as revealed in men's actions. Reason based not upon abstractions but upon these facts of human nature could eliminate everything from the products of the imagination which would not harmonize with them.

Besides affirming the necessity of imagination and reason in the creation of standards, Babbitt posited the existence of an almost mystical higher will which opposed the natural man expressed through the *élan vital*.[11] By asserting that this higher will could guide reason, Babbitt assured himself that the higher will would assist man to use his reason to reinforce the *frein vital*.

---

[9]Babbitt, *ibid.*, p. 295.

[10]Babbitt, *On Being Creative*, p. xxx.

[11]Although Babbitt himself believed in a humanist higher will, he admitted that it might also have a supernatural basis. This accounts in large part for the interest Roman Catholic writers have taken in him. See Russell Wilbur, "A Word About Babbitt," in *Commonweal*, Jan. 25, 1935, pp. 364-366; Dom Oliver Grosselin, *The Intuitive Voluntarism of Irving Babbitt* (Latrobe, Pa., 1951); Francis E. McMahan, *The Humanism of Irving Babbitt* (Washington, 1931); and Louis J. A. Mercier, *American Humanism and the New Age* (Milwaukee, 1948).

If university investigators would conduct research along these lines, Babbitt maintained, new standards would result which civilized men could transmit from generation to generation. Acting consciously, men in and out of the universities could discipline themselves and their children to act in accordance with the new standards. Their actions would then form new habits. In this manner, according to him, men could develop civilized traditions which would satisfy the needs of human nature because they would conform to the observed facts of that nature.

Unfortunately for the spread of Babbitt's ideas, he never linked his doctrines of the higher will, reason, and imagination to the psychological thought current in his day. In fact in all his writings, he never mentioned anything which would indicate he was aware of them. Instead of cooperating with or gently criticizing scholars like the psychologists, he attacked them and American higher education in general for neglecting the study of human nature. He felt that they were failing to look for the facts of human experience needed to establish the new standards required for the progress of civilization. He should not have dismissed the efforts of his contemporaries, for many scholars in the humanities and social sciences were studying human nature and society. Not only might they have become interested in his specific work, he might also have had a check on his own scholarship.

An Elitist Society of Standards

Babbitt condemned the direction undergraduate education had taken since the demise of the nineteenth-century literary college because of its lack of attention to the reinforcement of the *frein vital* within the students. Babbitt doubted that the men of character who were needed to assume positions of leadership in business, government, and the professions would emerge if American colleges and universities did not prepare them.

Babbitt maintained that only the few could ever live by good standards. In the vein of his Calvinist forebears, he believed that most men cannot control their lower nature. Adopting Matthew Arnold's phrase, he stated that civilization depends not upon the average man but upon the "saving remnant," that small number in which the *frein vital* controls the *élan vital*.[12] Since in his framework only those who have accepted the discipline of the higher will can restrain the expansive urges of the natural man, only they will be able to prevent society itself from running amuck. If the Remnant were to disappear, civilization would collapse because " . . . barbarism is always as close to the most refined civilization as rust is to the most highly polished steel."[13]

Babbitt further emphasized the need for men of standards in the twentieth century because of the decline of dogma and authority, which acted as checks upon the *élan vital* of a society. With the rise of a civilization in which the critical spirit prevailed, primitivists were attacking convention. The morality evinced by naturalists like Emile Zola and Theodore Dreiser only convinced Babbitt that primitivism was overwhelming civilization. He believed that the Remnant had to create new conventions if the ordinary people were to be saved from barbarism.

Babbitt believed that a great civilization in a sense is only a great tradition, but his great civilization would not be sterile and rigid because it would continually change its standards.[14] He stated that no convention is final and incapable of improvement. Through the use of will, imagination, and reason to create new standards, a society could avoid outmoded and burdensome traditions. As he put it, a "law of universal

---

[12]Irving Babbitt, *Democracy and Leadership* (Boston and New York, 1924), p. 278.

[13]Babbitt, *ibid.*, p. 229.

[14]Babbitt, *ibid.*, p. 301.

relativity" or a "oneness that is always changing" affects human life.[15] Babbitt's standards were to oppose the flux of popular, unrestrained impulse but retain their relevance by being based upon institutions and not upon abstract theories of any absolute. "Standards are a matter of observation and common sense, the absolute is only a metaphysical conceit."[16] Modern man needs not absolutes but an authority to which he can turn when all else is flux.

Surprisingly for a person who usually deprecated American institutions, Babbitt held up the United States Constitution as an example of the political authority he favored. In checking the *élan vital* of a democratic, expansive people, the Constitution does for the nation what the *frein vital* does for the individual. Corresponding to the dualism within each man, American constitutional democracy reflects a sound concept of human nature and thus works well. It allows for expansion but has the checks of a traditionalist society. He heartily approved of the conservative, formalistic interpretations of the Constitution rendered by the Supreme Court during his lifetime.

Babbitt continually emphasized that a nation needs men of tradition and character, not scientific intellectuals—or any intellectuals, including university professors—to rule if it is to prosper. Leaders who act in accord with standards serve as the counterpoise to the expansive urges within society. Even within a legal structure of checks and balances, only such leaders can limit and direct the people's sheer will to power which leads to the disruption of civilization.

Babbitt displayed, basically, a distrust of the people. Such political reforms as the direct election of senators, the referendum, and the initiative increased the power of the people over their government, and Babbitt decried these changes.

---

[15]Irving Babbitt, *Literature and the American College* (Chicago, 1956), p. 124. Babbitt, *Rousseau and Romanticism*, p. 7.

[16]Babbitt, *Democracy and Leadership*, p. 306.

Parliamentary government would not find new strength through such devices; it would become impossible. The people would place too much faith in themselves and lose respect not only for their leaders but for any authority.

After surveying the history of Greek and French democracy, he concluded that democracy becomes, practically, "standardized and commercialized melodrama."[17]   He believed that the progressive American leadership was putting too much faith in the common man and would "pass through disillusionment to a final despair."[18]   If America were not to reverse the trend represented by progressive legislation toward direct majority rule, its version of democracy would lead it to destruction.   He feared the unrestrained impulses of the populace.

He predicted that the drift in America toward unchecked democratic control would eliminate the leader loyal to sound standards.[19]   Babbitt approved of the democratic desire of equal opportunity for all only as long as it implied "that everybody is to have a chance to measure up to high standards."[20]   Then a democracy could produce individuals who look to standards above themselves.   If it does not, Babbitt feared that American democratic society would become an especially unpleasant way of returning to barbarism.[21]

As he viewed twentieth-century America, he did not see ethical leaders in possession of humane standards dominating the scene as they had in the early days of the Republic. Ignoring Theodore Roosevelt, William Howard Taft, and Woodrow Wilson, he stated that the new leaders like Warren Harding and Calvin Coolidge lacked the moral gravity and intellectual

---

[17]Babbitt, *ibid.,* p. 242.

[18]Babbitt, *ibid.,* p. 261.

[19]Babbitt, *ibid.,* p. 245.

[20]Babbitt, *ibid.,* p. 312.

[21]Babbitt, *Rousseau and Romanticism,* p. 286.

seriousness of George Washington, John Adams, Thomas Jefferson, James Madison, James Monroe, and John Quincy Adams.

American education was to blame for the decline of standards, Babbitt lamented. In attempting to satisfy social wishes, it was mistakenly educating students in techniques which would give them control of their objective environment but not over their own subjective needs. He fervently believed that contemporary educational practices were merely increasing the student's power to destroy civilization since it gave him control over nature but not over his own temperament.

Typically, he never brought forth evidence to indicate that the classical colleges actually had been more effective in developing character. He simply relied upon his intuition and criticized contemporary higher education without any firm empirical evidence. He never followed his own plan for arriving at valid positions by testing intuitive knowledge with hard facts. He did not even come to grips with the extent to which formal education is responsible for personal standards and to what degree other personal forces are responsible. He frequently mentioned that in the past Puritanism had provided the indispensable check on the American. Yet he failed to deal with the question central to any consideration of the relationship between education and society. To what degree had education influenced society, and to what degree had society influenced education? If in the past Puritanism had provided the needed check upon the *élan vital* of the country, what role had education played in the process? Could formal education of any variety be expected to substitute for the loss of general beliefs among the population at large?

The Evil of Humanitarianism

In the midst of a progressive America passing laws to remedy social ills, Babbitt condemned the reform movement as not only futile but actually destructive. Reformers, he maintained, failed to recognize that the struggle between good and evil best takes place within the heart of each individual. Transferring this battle to society, he observed, blinds men to the realization that wars and social injustice stem from the unharmonious relationship within each man between the *frein vital* and the *élan vital*.

He reasoned that contemporary legislation came from a sympathy divorced from a realistic appraisal of human nature. Babbitt approved of the social pity which gave rise to much of the reform movement but lamented that the conflict between the *élan vital* and the *frein vital* within each man had been forgotten.[22] He did not want the Christian virtue of love for one's neighbor as seen in many reformers to find expression in impersonal policies and thus take the place of individual repentance and regeneration. Christian stalwarts like Paul or Augustine, he commented, would call social reformers "weaklings and degenerates."[23] The two saints would not have mistaken easily implemented state reforms as an adequate substitute for the hard task of individual conversion to correct principles of living.

After reflecting upon the reform movement, Babbitt pronounced it a "monstrous legalism" resulting from the attempt to deal with evil socially rather than at its source in the individual. He held that political reforms actually result in more rather than less injustice because they detract attention from the crucial issue: the balance between the *élan vital* and the *frein vital*. Moreover, every form of social legislation undermines moral standards because it substitutes force for them.

Giving expression to his elitism, Babbitt stated that if he were called upon to remedy the social evils of American life, he would place his faith "in the moderation and magnanimity of the strong and the successful, and not in any sickly sentimen-

---

[22]Babbitt, *Literature and the College*, p. 43.

[23]Babbitt, *ibid.*, p. 7.

talizing over the lot of the underdog."[24] Only the beneficence of properly educated leaders would bring justice into the world. Only the moral realist, as he classified himself, comprehended that the struggle between good and evil within each man could not be shifted to society. Not reform, but humanistic education of the elite, provided the key to the solution of society's ills.

Babbitt believed that submission to the discipline of humane standards would lead to a fulfillment of the dream of human progress.[25] In his opinion, endless schemes for uplifting the common man would fail. Only the increased power of men of standards would bring justice. He reiterated that the humanitarian legalist passes innumerable laws for the control of people who refuse to control themselves.[26] Those in control of the nation seemed to be enjoying the illusion of reforming society instead of setting to the sober task of strengthening individual ethical standards.

A paradox, however, existed in this desire for elite leadership and Babbitt's condemnation of the reformers. On one hand he called for the restrictions which his leaders, in conformity with higher standards, would impose on the population. On the other hand, he bitterly condemned regulations to control antisocial behavior. He criticized Supreme Court rulings upholding legislation on working conditions of women and children, and he opposed Congressional legislation on white slavery. To be sure, Babbitt did not condone the exploitation of women and children or the existence of prostitution. He believed such conditions were evil. Yet he failed to explain why national leaders, even if they were not his elite, should not impose proper restraints upon the people. Wouldn't his elite have to take similar action?

---

[24]Babbitt, *Democracy and Leadership,* p. 205.

[25]Babbitt, *Literature and the College,* p. 174.

[26]Babbitt, *On Being Creative,* p. 210.

Strength of Giants and Intelligence of Children

Although not condemning technological power itself, Babbitt did not believe that scientific findings had given mankind answers to supreme moral issues; they had only intensified the importance of such matters. America, he feared, was in danger "of combining the strength of giants with the critical intelligence of children."[27] He warned that efficient megalomaniacs would not only destroy one another; they would also do the same to the meek who are supposed to inherit the earth.

Years before the First World War, Babbitt was convinced that the material power of men had moved ahead of their wisdom. Americans, he lamented, appear ignorant. Although they were not fools, they were reading just the things fools would read: comics and cheap magazines. Indeed, he thought he had witnessed the substitution of the comic book for the Bible.[28]

The breakdown of traditional Christian values, combined with man's increased control over the forces of nature, was creating madmen who could order the use of terrible means of destruction.[29] With some prescience, he predicted in a vein reminiscent of Henry Adams that man might well succeed in releasing the power of the atom only to destroy himself. Higher education shared part of this blame, for it had helped to increase man's control of his environment.

---

[27]Babbitt, *Democracy and Leadership*, p. 282.

[28]Babbitt, *Literature and the College*, p. 43.

[29]Babbitt, *Democracy and Leadership*, p. 143.

THE IMPORTANCE OF HIGHER EDUCATION

One is at all events safe in affirming that the battle that is to determine the fate of American civilization will be fought out first of all in the field of education.[30]

As Babbitt reflected upon the American scene, he concluded that education was crucial for the future of the country. He believed that a nation uses education to create and transmit its values. He personally held that colleges and universities are the prime institutions for accomplishing this. Therefore he warned that the degeneration of institutions of higher education, even more than that of the theater, press, and popular novel, posed the greatest danger facing American civilization. The desire to make colleges and universities operationally useful to contemporary society spelled disaster for the country. Because of his negative view toward governmental reforms, he viewed the efforts of faculty members to provide advice to civil government as misdirected and ill advised. He worried more, however, about the shift within colleges and universities from concern with the subjective value structure within the individual to the concern with the objective, contemporary world.

Babbitt feared that the voluminous mass of information in American academic disciplines might well be burying the imagination, reflection, and inner energy necessary to create values. Since the rise of Germanic scholarship, scholars in all fields appeared to him to be grubbing for facts rather than searching for the cultural standards so badly needed by Western man. He thought these facts had no relevance to humanist standards and hence had nothing to do with true education. Education in his view implied the possession of standards and their transmission to the young. Scholarship was to serve as its handmaiden.

---

[30]Irving Babbitt, "Humanism: An Essay at Definition," in Foerster, *Humanism and America,* p. 51.

Genuine Positivism and the Past

Babbitt felt that German scholarship with its emphasis upon factual research and specialization had worked against moral progress primarily because it had diverted attention from human values. According to him, the adherents of German scholarship like Charles W. Eliot looked upon man not as an end in himself but as an instrument for attaining other goals. They had idealized progress in objective knowledge without regard for man's need for values. Babbitt therefore opposed research into areas unrelated to cultural standards.

The facts Babbitt wanted scholars to study were those of human nature. More specifically, he wanted scholars to study the manner of men's actions as revealed in the past. Man can observe the manner in which his ancestors actually lived. Then he can compare what he has found to the creative findings of the imagination. Babbitt's standards would consist of those creations of the imagination which corresponded to man's past actions. Babbitt pointed out that most so-called positivists are actually incomplete positivists because they reject the greater part of mankind's experiences when they repudiate the study of the past.

Babbitt's subjective approach to knowledge separated him from the main body of contemporary American scholarship. Most professors studied the subject matter of the natural sciences, the social sciences, or even most phases of the humanities in an objective fashion. Babbitt's use of the imagination, on the other hand, made his scholarly approach radically subjective. In emphasizing the importance of studying the past, Babbitt was not setting himself apart from all other academic men. His proposals about the use of imagination to discover constants in man's nature, however, differed sharply with the main currents of twentieth-century American academic endeavor.

He strongly attacked his highly regarded fellow Harvard faculty member, William James. James' relativism denied the importance of such constants. To relativists like William James and John Dewey, Babbitt replied that no one had disproved the existence of characteristics common to all men regardless of time and place. He admitted that local and relative circumstances influence the human condition and make all cultural patterns appear relative. On the other hand, he countered, no one had shown that the conventions prevailing in the past actually had conflicted with one another.[31] They might indeed not be relative. He himself never spelled out these enduring principles of man's nature but instead implored scholars to turn their attention to the search for them. If America failed to establish a viable civilization, he said, the blame would rest in scholarship's failure to search for new cultural standards which could serve as an expression of the constants in man's nature.

If this experiment shows signs of breaking down, the explanation is surely that it has failed thus far to achieve adequate equivalents for the traditional controls.[32]

To Produce Men of Quality

In commenting upon higher education, Babbitt pointed out that the college had the special responsibility for perpetuating the humane standards necessary for the continuation of civilization. The secondary school would deal with preparatory training and the university would search for cultural standards, but the college was to develop a balance between the *élan vital* and the *frein vital* in its students. The proper general education could do this. Babbitt thought the American college could instill in its students the goal of liking and disliking "the right things."[33] To do this he wanted it

---

[31]Babbitt, *Spanish Character,* p. 202.

[32]Babbitt, *Democracy and Leadership,* p. 238.

[33]Babbitt, "Humanism: An Essay at Definition," p. 43.

*to supply principles of taste and judgment . . . to give back-
ground and perspective, and inspire, if not the spirit of
conformity, at least a proper respect for the past experience of
the world.*[34]

The college should realize, Babbitt insisted, that its task
is to produce men adhering to standards. By concentrating on
this goal it could act as a check upon what he believed to be
the basically expansive nature of a democracy.

Instead of focusing upon the establishment of standards,
however, most programs of undergraduate education were
structured toward operational utility. Most curricula did not
deal with humanistic standards. Generally, they gave students
the opportunity to acquire knowledge which would be useful
later in life. As is clear from Babbitt's social views, he could
not conceive that a curriculum designed for operational utility
would result in the acquisition of standards by the students.

*The new education (I am speaking, of course, of the main
trend) . . . suggests rather a radical break with our traditional
ethos. The old education was, in intention at least, a training
for wisdom and character. The new education has been
summed up by President Eliot in the phrase: training for
service and power. We are all coming together more and
more in this idea of service. But, though service is supplying
us in a way with a convention, it is not, in either the humanistic or the religious sense, supplying us with standards. In
the current sense of the word it tends rather to undermine
standards.*[35]

In his philosophy not utility or service but humanistic
standards poised an effective counter to the pursuit of
unethical power.

---

[34]Babbitt, *Literature and the College*, p. 162.

[35]Babbitt, *Democracy and Leadership*, p. 303.

In part he was correct, too, in voicing his concern for the fate of subjective values. As Rush Welter has aptly observed, the American faith in education was shifting during Babbitt's lifetime from an assurance that education would produce men capable of defining laudable social goals, to one of confidence only in education's ability to increase a man's technical efficiency.[36] If a good life does exist and standards can help men reach it, education should assist men to establish those standards.

Babbitt admitted that training for service has incidental advantages, but he wanted collegiate education to center upon personal values, not service. In the light of late-twentieth-century political history perhaps he was not altogether wrong, for he stated that:

The eager efforts of our philanthropists to do something for the negro and the newsboy are well enough in their way; but a society that hopes to be saved by what it does for its negroes and its newsboys is a society that is trying to lift itself by its own boot-straps. Our real hope of safety lies in our being able to induce our future Harrimans and Rockefellers to liberalize their own souls, in other words to get themselves rightly educated. Men of heroic capacity such as Messrs. Rockefeller and Harriman have in some respects shown themselves to be are, of course, born, not made; but when once born it will depend largely whether they are to become heroes of good or heroes of evil. We are told that the aim of Socrates in his training to the young was not to make them efficient, but to inspire in them reverence and restraint; for to make them efficient, said Socrates, without reverence and restraint, was simply to equip them with ampler means for harm.[37]

---

[36]Welter, *Popular Education and Democratic Thought*, pp. 325 ff.

[37]Babbitt, *Literature and the College*, pp. 47 ff.

Unfortunately Babbitt failed to perceive that future men of heroic capacity, like the Rockefellers, Harrimans, and Kennedys in the 1960's, would become heroes of good by using state power. And they would use it in just the way he condemned: by substituting legal force for individual inner restraint. His position would be represented by men like Barry Goldwater, Ronald Reagan, and George Wallace, hardly conforming to his ideal of the educated man.

Specialization

In Babbitt's view, the old classical education had assumed that men need to be disciplined to humanist standards. He lamented that the complexities of twentieth-century society demanded specialists to deal with them and thus reinforced tendencies toward specialization within the academic world. As a result, not study of the values needed for good living but fact grubbing in esoteric fields had become the way to academic promotion.

The detailed specialization of twentieth-century scholarship, he complained, threatened to turn erudition into pedantry and encouraged pure dilettantism in the field of values. He pointed, for example, to the German Ph.D. degree. Too mechanical and specialized, it rejected the broad traditions of man. According to his observation, one might satisfy the requirements for it with brilliant, narrow research but still lack the insight and reflection requisite to unify subject matter so important for the humanistic studies. In short, he did not see how it could supply the training necessary for the development of the teachers needed to strengthen the *frein vital.*

He suggested that a new degree requiring broad reading and understanding be substituted for the Ph.D.

Such distinctions as a First Class in an Oxford honor school or the French agrégation *would not in themselves be suited to our needs; but they at least illustrate how a degree that*

stands primarily for reading and assimilation may be made
as severe and searching as a degree that stands primarily for
research. . . . Who can doubt that a teacher of French who
had thus widely read in the ancient and modern classics
would be of more use to the average college than the man
who had demonstrated his "originality" by collecting examples
of the preposition in Old French from Godefroy's Dictionary?
Or that the classical scholar who knew his Plato and Aristotle
both in themselves and in their relation to the humane
tradition of the world would do more to advance his subject
than the man who had devoted painful vigils to writing a
thesis on the uses of dum, donec, *and* quoad?[38]

To a great extent, Babbitt had just cause to complain,
for the new doctoral recipients coming forth from the graduate
schools of the country were neglecting broad reading and good
teaching in favor of specialized research leading to publication.
If need be, all too many of them would slight their students in
order to cultivate the regard of their colleagues who might
read and hopefully praise their books and articles. Babbitt,
however, failed to devise an alternative program for training
collegiate instructors. He could only assert that the search for
standards would create a civilization which would produce the
needed leaders of the modern age.

Babbitt's feelings on this matter were perhaps intensified
because of his own position. He himself had refused to work
for a Ph.D. At Harvard, he fought with the philologists oriented
to esoteric factual research and ridiculed their scientific approach
to the study of literature. In turn, they disapproved of him.
At the beginning of his career, they had prevented his receiving
a desired appointment to the classics department, and only the
support of some distinguished students prevented his removal
from the university altogether.

---

[38]Babbitt, *ibid.,* pp. 94-95.

Not possessing an especially endearing personality, Babbitt had given his colleagues cause for animosity. He said that they did not possess the wisdom necessary to impart values to their students. He had maintained that the humanities should be interpreted by men of broad reading, not by specialists in fields he felt inappropriate to specialization. Declaring that Harvard faculty members did not lack humanistic traits, he asserted that those traits simply did not predominate in them. The academic men around him could not use imagination and reason to penetrate facts, organize them, and relate them to the present. In spite of the important work which Harvard faculty members like Josiah Royce and William James were doing, Babbitt remarked that professors were neglecting the formation of the minds and characters of young men who should be leading all segments of society.[39]

With perhaps more justification, Babbitt observed that the specialists about him like George Lyman Kittredge, chairman of the department of comparative literature, were too absorbed in attaining eminence in their academic disciplines to relate their findings "to the total harmony of life."[40] Kittredge, for example, devoted much attention to esoteric philological subjects. In a sense American scholarship in the humanities did indeed depreciate reflective scholarship, disregard the broad historical approach to literary analysis, and rely instead upon novel ideas.

Not only specialization on the professorial level disturbed Babbitt. If the colleges were to strengthen the *frein vital* in a humane leadership, they would have to concentrate upon a small number of subjects of no operational utility. Instead, in an effort to allow their students to acquire knowledge of operational utility, they generally had adopted various forms of the elective principle. Babbitt, thinking that no form of

---

[39]Babbitt, *ibid.,* p. 119.

[40]Irving Babbitt, *Humanist and Specialist* (Providence, 1926), p. 7.

elective system provides the necessary restraint upon the student's *élan vital,* observed that at Harvard many students simply took the easiest courses.

Having provided such a rich and costly banquet of electives to satisfy the "infinite variety" of youths of eighteen, President Eliot must be somewhat disappointed to see how nearly all these youths insist on flocking into a few large courses; and especially disappointed that many of them should take advantage of the elective system not to work strenuously along the line of their special interests, but rather to lounge through their college course along the line of least resistance. A popular philosopher has said that every man is as lazy as he dares to be. If he had said that nine men in ten are as lazy as they dare to be, he would have come near hitting a great truth.[41]

Thus Babbitt objected to the elective principle because it did not conform to his view of human nature: i.e., men need discipline. Possessing no *frein vital,* most students would follow the impulses of the *élan vital* and have a good time.

Elective systems would not discipline the student with the proper subjects. Babbitt wanted material illustrative of the constants in human nature to be the heart of collegiate education. He thought that the Greek classics fused reason and imagination, the ingredients of humanistic standards, better than any other subject. Hence, the bulk of the curriculum should consist of them. They would provide the proper education for American youth.

. . . it is the Greek writers who best show the modern mind the path that it needs to take; for the modern man cannot, like the man of the Middle Ages, live by the imagination and religious faculty alone; on the other hand, he cannot live solely by the exercise of his reason and understanding. It is

---

[41]Babbitt, *Literature and the College,* pp. 35-36.

*only by the union of these two elements of his nature that
he can hope to attain a balanced growth, and this fusion of
the reason and the imagination is found realized more perfectly than elsewhere in the Greek classics of the great age.*[42]

As he looked back upon the classical curriculum of the
American literary college, he reasoned that it had embodied the
seasoned and matured experience of a multitude of men, extending over a considerable time. The Greece of Plato, Socrates,
and the Sophists remains an excellent object of study for the
modern world. Losing its cultural standards, it followed the
course which he feared America to be treading.

*The critical moment of Greek life was, like the present, a
period of naturalistic emancipation, when the multitude was
content to live without standards, and the few were groping
for inner standards to take the place of the outer standards
they had lost. The Greek problems were like our own,
problems of unrestraint; for what we see on every hand in
our modern society, when we get beneath the veneer of scientific progress, is barbaric violation of the law of measure.
Greek society perished, as our modern society may very well
perish, from an excess of naturalism. . . . Therefore both in
its failures and its success, Greece, especially the Greece of
Socrates and Plato and the Sophists, is rich in instruction
for us,—more so, I am inclined to think than any other period
of the past whatsoever. This is the very moment that we
are choosing to turn away from the study of Greek. One
might suppose that before deserting the* exemplaria graeca
*it would be wiser to wait until the world has another age that
proves as clearly as did the great age of Greece that man may
combine an exquisite measure with a perfect spontaneity, that
he may be at once thoroughly disciplined and roughly inspired.*[43]

---

[42]Babbitt, *ibid.*, pp. 120-121.

[43]Irving Babbitt, *The New Laokoon* (Boston, 1910), pp. 251-252.

Rather than approve the prevailing trend in American undergraduate instruction toward vocational courses or general education of an immediate, factual nature, Babbitt denounced it. In his mind, the justification for American higher education lay in the strengthening of the *frein vital* in the students who would become the leaders in a society with no restrictions upon them other than their own sense.

He feared that American colleges and universities were failing in their responsibility.

> *The older education aimed to produce leaders and, as it perceived, the basis of leadership is not commercial or industrial efficiency, but wisdom. Those who have been substituting the cult of efficiency for the older liberal training are, of course, profuse in their professions of service either to country or to mankind at large.*[44]

He did not think that service, in its humanitarian sense, could serve as an effective counterpoise to the pursuit of unethical power. Only the cultivation of the *frein vital* could accomplish that.

In Babbitt's opinion, college alumni proved his assertion that American higher education was failing to develop men of standards. He thought that they presented a sorry picture. With some correctness, he pointed out that during their leisure, they are indistinguishable from men of affairs without a college education. Looking at their habits of reading, Babbitt concluded that the colleges and universities were as effective as "an immense whir of machinery in the void."[45]

---

[44]Babbitt, *Democracy and Leadership*, p. 304.

[45]Irving Babbitt, "The Breakdown of Internationalism," *Nation*, June 24, 1915, p. 706.

Higher Education and Standards

Unfortunately for his case, Babbitt failed to provide evidence that the classical college had indeed functioned as he claimed. He really never grounded any of his theories about man, society, and education in the very facts which he insisted formed the basis of reputable scholarship. In deprecating the collegiate graduate, for instance, he never made any controlled study of American college and university alumni. He simply made his judgment upon the basis of random personal observations. In all his other criticisms of American education, politics, and society, he followed the same method. Essentially a literary critic, he simply referred to the subjective writings of other men which do not in themselves constitute a direct record of the actions of men. He neglected to study the economic and social forces transforming the universities.

Perhaps his basically subjective approach to life itself accounts for his disapproval of higher education for utility. The new education removed the development of individual subjective standards as the *raison d'être* of the American college. While Babbitt considered these all-important, the advocates of higher education for operational utility would concentrate the energies of faculty and students upon the objective world, both natural and social.

The new curricular developments thus appeared ill advised to him. The new vocational orientation of much of the undergraduate program at most colleges and universities was of course irrelevant to Babbitt's aims for education. The nature of the curriculum which had been established in response to the changing conditions in American society appeared short sighted and foolish to a man whose central concern lay in the strengthening of the *frein vital.*

Self-expression and vocational training combined in various proportions and tempered by the spirit of "service" are nearly the whole of the new education. But I have already said that it is not possible to extract from any such compounding of utilitarian and romantic elements, with the resulting material efficiency and ethical inefficiency, a civilized view of life.[46]

Babbitt's basic criticism of contemporary American higher education, then, does not rest primarily in the fact that colleges and universities were responding to societal needs. Rather, his argument rests upon a difference of opinion concerning the real needs of society.

What is wanted is not training for service and training for power, but training for wisdom and training for character.[47]

Essentially the proponents of education for operational utility assumed that man in fact needs more control over his material and social environment. Hence they furthered the role of the natural and social sciences in higher education. Babbitt, on the other hand, did not agree with them.

What is important in man in the eyes of the humanist is not his power to act on the world, but his power to act upon himself.[48]

Unfortunately for Babbitt's whole educational critique, no one knows for sure whether formal education can result in humane standards for either the individual or his society. Who can prove that the graduates of the nineteenth-century literary college in fact acted with more restraint than the graduates of the twentieth-century university? Even if it could be substantiated, how certain can those in charge of educational

---

[46]Babbitt, *Rousseau and Romanticism,* p. 293.

[47]Babbitt, *Literature and the College,* p. 46.

[48]Babbitt, *ibid.,* p. 37.

policy be that Babbitt's vague proposals would actually affect character more positively than a curriculum of operational utility?

In relying upon education alone to develop character, he exhibited a remarkable faith in education. He did not appreciate the role of the family, church, and community. If these institutions are more important than formal education in enculturating the young, the undergraduate curriculum would not have been crucial for the maintenance of societal standards. His concern about a university's responsibility in the creation of new cultural standards is another matter, but nevertheless, his ideas demand a naive faith in the ability of reason to change traditions of belief and value.

These objections should not detract from the importance of Babbitt's central message: the necessity for standards. His criticisms of higher education may or may not be valid, but his concern is legitimate. Without men of character, even the most elaborately structured society cannot function for the welfare of all. Babbitt at least affirmed that men could find and adopt individual and social standards.

Still, all universities should not have to drop their concern for vocational training, reorient all their research toward the creation of standards, and focus their general education upon the inculcation of these standards in order to deal with Babbitt's concerns. The country need not adopt his monist viewpoint about the function of American colleges and universities. America should have the economic and human resources to develop both power and morality. No one has yet shown them to be mutually exclusive.

If men continue to extend their control over the physical world without mastering the principles of their own nature, they may destroy themselves as Babbitt warned. The nation desperately needs leaders of wisdom and character, and American colleges and universities should be working to develop them.

To a generation threatened with atomic annihilation, Babbitt's premonitions of destruction do not appear foolish.

Nevertheless, he should not be excused from his failure to deal with the issue of meeting society's current operational problems. In his critique of higher education he neglected to consider the relationship between operational complexities and the improvement of society. By objecting to education directed toward operational utility, he implied that operationally useful education is unimportant. Even if his elite came into being, it would have to control effective operational devices in order to create a better society. Faced with contemporary operational problems, could those responsible for higher education ignore the preparation needed to cope with them? In perhaps more practical terms, would those responsible for financing American colleges and universities allow them to neglect education of operational utility? In fact they have not, and Babbitt's warnings go unheeded.

CHAPTER FOUR

ALBERT JAY NOCK:
Apostle of Despair

The well-disposed persons whom I saw hopefully relying on education to bring about world-peace, to achieve some semblance of a civilised society, or to fulfill some other gradiose collective purpose, were leaning on a broken staff.

ALBERT JAY NOCK, 1943

ALBERT JAY NOCK represented the pessimistic American elitist tradition characterized by Henry Adams and Ralph Adams Cram. Although he shared Babbitt's strong sense of tradition, he did not share Babbitt's basic optimism that the course of education or American society could be improved by rational efforts. Nock concluded that the destruction of the classical college had signified the end of a viable American culture. Convinced that a materialistic society dominated its institutions of higher learning, he could not conceive that it would allow them to deviate from established societal norms. He thus viewed as inevitable the functioning of colleges and universities in response to the immediate wishes of state legislators and wealthy donors. Higher education for operational utility was to be expected. In his opinion the instrumental nature of colleges and universities was simply a result of outside interest groups wishing a return on their investment.

At the foundation of his mature, published thought lay a firm conviction that the overwhelming majority of men were little more than animals. He therefore decried contemporary attempts to educate the populace. Neither larger numbers of students nor success of extension programs in reaching the general population necessarily indicates an advance of civilization, and Nock recognized this fact. If his assumption about most modern men representing something between the apes and humane individuals is accepted, the conclusion logically follows that a close relationship between colleges and universities and their social environments would not enhance the quality of higher education. In fact he pointed out that society had destroyed education.

Nock did not think that the domination of American society by what he called crude, materialistic men could be reversed, and hence his career represents a paradox. Asserting that societal trends could not be overcome through conscious effort, why did he bother to write? He knew that his ideas fell outside the mainstream of American life and thought, and he did not note any possibility of their being adopted. Perhaps he only desired to write for intellectual pleasure and satisfaction, for some men must express their discontent. His writings indicate his appreciation of controversy and colorful rhetoric. At any rate, he spent most of his time urging a change in conditions which he maintained could not be changed.

Nock's view of himself probably contributed to the strengthening of his elitist position. In his autobiography, *Memoirs of a Superfluous Man,* he claimed that during all his life he had

---

[1]In Albert Jay Nock, *Journal of Forgotten Days, May* 1934-*October* 1935 (Hinsdale, Ill., 1948), *Foreword,* Nock's children report that shortly before he died, he destroyed all his manuscripts and notes except this posthumously published diary. Moreover, during his lifetime he refused to give information about his personal life to even a publication so innocuous as *Who's Who in America.* He considered his personal affairs to be private. Thus knowledge of his life remains sketchy. Even his *Memoirs* reveal little about him other than his ideas.

stood above the common people.[1] Born in 1870 into an Episcopal clergyman's household, he spent his earliest days in Brooklyn, New York, where he received every opportunity to mature in accord with the sanctions of lofty taste and manners. In the Brooklyn of his day he was surrounded by cultivated conversation and good books. After the age of ten, he moved with his parents to Alpena, Michigan, but even there he received the typical classical education.

The college he attended, St. Stephen's, was ideally situated for developing a dislike of urban mass civilization. Now known as Bard College, St. Stephen's lay somewhat isolated on the shores of the Hudson River about one hundred miles north of New York City. In 1890, with a faculty of eight, it enrolled eighty-one students and required a classical course of study, the hallmark of leisure-class education.

As a boy Nock had spurned the classics, thinking them proper only for stuffed shirts, but four years of reading Greek and Latin literature convinced him that this alone constituted a proper education. Hence any twentieth-century university which spurned the unitary study of the classics was not educating its students. Since the state universities and even colleges like Harvard and Yale were devoting most of their attention to subjects unrelated to Greek and Latin, he concluded that their graduates were uneducated.

Nock's experiences after graduation in 1892 remain somewhat unclear, but apparently he taught Latin and Greek at St. Stephen's from 1896 to 1898. He then served as an Episcopal minister until 1909, when he left the ministry because of his loss of faith in Christianity. After that he worked on the *American Magazine* until 1914, and he devoted most of the rest of his life to writing.[2]

---

[2]Robert M. Crunden, *The Mind and Art of Albert Jay Nock* (Chicago, 1964). This Yale Senior Thesis traces the events of Nock's life more fully than any other published work. See it for further details about Nock's activities.

From 1920 to 1924 he edited perhaps the most literate contemporary periodical in the United States, *The Freeman*. Its editorials, tinged with Nock's advocacy of anarchism, placed him among the best known intellectuals of the day. Firmly believing in the free exchange of ideas, he encouraged writers with a wide range of views to publish in *The Freeman*. Along with thinkers like William Z. Foster, Howard Mumford Jones, Lewis Mumford, John Dos Passos, and Lincoln Steffens, he criticized the unintelligent, uninspired American ethos epitomized by men like Harding and Coolidge.[3] Like these writers, he found much to debunk in America.

During the 1920's and 1930's he maintained a personal friendship with Henry L. Mencken of *The American Mercury,* and he used the *Mercury's* columns to denounce government at all levels. He liked the magazine's style of criticism and felt at home with Mencken's friends.[4] He agreed with them that America was a miserable place for any person of culture and refinement.

Upon the coming of the New Deal, Nock continued to preach his individualistic ideology and sympathized with the conservative opposition to Franklin Roosevelt. In 1934 he considered working for the American Liberty League. Although Nock considered its members philistines, they represented a hope to crush the growing power of a government controlled by a population devoid of intelligence. Since the conservatives would restrict the prerogatives of government, the few men of culture and learning within American society might at least be spared the enervating influence of an all-pervasive control by the masses.[5]

---

[3]See Susan J. Turner, *A History of The Freeman* (New York, 1963) .

[4]Nock, *Journal of Forgotten Days*, pp. 12-13; *Letters from Albert Jay Nock, 1924-1945, to Edmund C. Evans, Mrs. Edmund C. Evans, and Ellen Winsor* (Caldwell, Idaho, 1949) , p. 190.

[5]Nock, *Journal of Forgotten Days*, p. 45.

During the 1930's he returned professionally to education and in 1931 accepted a position as Visiting Professor of Politics and American History at St. Stephen's College, by then a branch of Columbia University and soon to be renamed Bard College. It had an enrollment of less than three hundred and still followed the general educational plan of the nineteenth-century American literary college. Considering this program essentially sound, he wanted to observe it to find out if indeed any hope remained of educating the intelligent. He did not remain long. After two years he left, convinced that education could not mitigate the other forces of society.

During Nock's entire life his interest in higher education never failed, but with his view of the average man, he could not foresee the improvement of a democratic society through education. In contrast to Babbitt, who had believed that education could make a significant contribution by defining cultural standards and by building character in students, Nock stated that the forces of mass democracy had overwhelmed the nineteenth-century tradition of nonoperational education. Like Babbitt, Nock wanted men of culture and refinement to rule as they did in the day of Adams and Jefferson, but he saw no hope for colleges and universities to produce these men until properly educated men ruled. Until that time, society would require colleges and universities to emphasize subjects which would prepare the student for operating in society rather than for becoming a better person.

To the end of his days, Nock could find no sign that conditions would change. He himself had never drawn any kind of a following. Since he considered himself one of the few American men of culture, he could not foresee much hope that the right kind of men would gain power. In 1943, two years before his death, he wrote in his autobiography that men of refinement, including himself, were superfluous. A society which placed faith in the majority of men would not easily recognize that civilization advanced not through a reliance upon the will of the people but, as Jefferson stated, through the guidance of a natural elite of wisdom and character.

Instead of developing its natural elite, Nock complained, America was neglecting the educable and forcing its colleges and universities to attempt to raise the understanding of everyone. In his opinion, only the select few should gain admission to colleges and universities, for only they possessed the capability to benefit from education. He even toyed with the idea that the rest of the people might be happiest if left illiterate. Their inferiority would then be plain to them, and they would follow the naturally gifted leaders of society.

THE ELITE SOCIETY

Neanderthal Man and the Remnant

Nock agreed with John Adams that most men do not give a tinker's damn about anything other than their dinner and their girl. They care nothing about civilization. Nock even said that most creatures commonly known as *homo sapiens* are in fact neither civilized nor human. He believed that most of them were closer to Neanderthal man than to men of character and wisdom. The difference between a Socrates and a man of the crowd, he averred, is greater than that between a man of the crowd and an ape. Adopting the phrase of his friend, Ralph Adams Cram, he often referred to most men as Neolithic.

Nock's ideas about society paralleled those of Babbitt because both condemned the notion that a society should operate upon the assumption that all men are equal. They both believed that some men by nature are superior to others. In fact both even used the same word of Matthew Arnold to refer to the elite group: the Remnant; and they both separated society into two segments called the Remnant and the Masses.

Nock, however, did not base his division between the Remnant and the Masses upon the relationship between the *frein vital* and the *élan vital*. Instead he relied far more directly upon the intellect. He gave it equal standing with character. Babbitt had believed that intellect was a necessary factor in creating and accepting standards but stressed the role of habit in adhering to them. Nock, on the other hand, saw in reason the means by which the Remnant could overcome the bounds of its cultural conditioning. In short, they both maintained that character was necessary, but Nock relied more upon thinking than did Babbitt, who primarily trusted good habits.

Both of them took the position that personal standards of behavior were far more important than a person's ability to act in the world of affairs. Operational utility appeared irrelevant in both of their conceptions of the good life. The differentiating features between a member of the Remnant and of the Masses lay not in a man's ability to operate efficiently but in his inward personal characteristics.

Nock defined the Masses, in part, in light of their ability to think. Mass-men, he stated, feel rather than think. They accept the institutions into which they are born as one does the atmosphere; "one's practical adjustments to it are made by a kind of reflex."[6] Nock asserted that their very sense of life and the convictions proceeding from it come from their experience alone. He completely accepted an unnamed study of soldiers made during World War I. It revealed that the intelligence of the average soldier equalled that of a twelve year old. Nock used this information to bolster his assertion that the Masses cannot think for themselves. The Masses might have the ability to be trained, to compare relationships, and even to rearrange ideas. They lack, however, the ability to apprehend correct principles of life and fail in the character needed to use these principles as modes for living.

---

[6]Albert Jay Nock, *Our Enemy, the State* (New York, 1935), p. 30.

*The mass-man is one who has neither the force of intellect
to apprehend the principles issuing in what we know as the
humane life, nor the force of character to adhere to those
principles steadily and strictly as laws of conduct; and because
such people make up the great, the overwhelming majority
of mankind, they are called collectively the masses. . . . The
Remnant are those who by force of character are able, at least
measurably, to cleave to them; the masses are those who are
unable to do either.*[7]

Nock believed that only the Remnant, not the Masses, could
plan for the future. The Masses could not immunize themselves
from the irritating influences of hunger, lust, and jealously for
a long-range point of view because they could not think. Unlike
Babbitt, Nock explained that tradition or the atmosphere in
which they lived could not protect them because new conditions
of life continually arise which demand thinking. An educational
program ignoring the development of the Remnant and concentrating upon operational knowledge for everyone thus ran
counter to Nock's views of social goals.

He attacked the notion that everyone is educable and
decried attempts to educate the general population. Any kind
of educational program designed to raise the level of understanding of the Masses through direct means was ill conceived.
Efforts to increase the Masses' control of their environment were
bound not only to fail but to create worse problems because
those efforts enabled the Masses to exercise power beyond their
ability and will to control it.[8]

Man's Archenemy: The State

As Nock viewed the functioning of the state, he concluded
that mankind had periodically fallen into war and chaos

---

[7]Albert Jay Nock, *Free Speech and Plain Language* (New York, 1937),
p. 251.

[8]Albert Jay Nock, *The Theory of Education in the United States* (New
York, 1932), pp. 30 ff.

because men who could not think ruled the state.[9]   In more than mere jest, Nock asked himself how a nation could ever move toward a civilization based upon humane values if the leaders were really not human.   Not reason and understanding, but force was the only tool he could envision them using.   They could not grasp anything else.   Education geared to useful knowledge had simply failed to produce the kind of leadership the nation required.

As he considered the ideals and aspirations of those he called the Masses, he lamented that no one had stopped them from putting their stamp upon the nation itself.   Like Babbitt, he concluded that they had made America a dreary place.   A nation of "shabbiness, meanness, childishness, and spiritual poverty" had resulted from the rule by a majority of "bumptious and turbulent twelve-year-olds."[10]   Nock, viewing the condition of American civilization, could only smile at "the current sublimated drivel about the preciousness of 'democracy.' "[11]

Nock opposed the regulatory and welfare services of the state even as limited as they were during the 1920's. Maintaining that the American populace lacked the mentality to order its passions and control its instinct for blind action, he said that the government had fallen into the hands of sagacious knaves seeking their own economic advantage.   This belief fit directly into his theory of the state, for he condemned the very existence

---

[9]His books dealing directly with the role of the state include: *Myth of a Guilty Nation* (New York, 1922) and *Our Enemy, the State*.   Moreover, *Jefferson* (New York, 1926) ; *On Doing the Right Thing and Other Essays* (New York, 1928) ; *The Book of Journeyman* (New York, 1930) ; *Free Speech and Plain Language; Henry George* (New York, 1939) ; and *Memoirs of a Superfluous Man* (New York, 1943) all devote considerable attention to the state's functioning.

[10]Albert Jay Nock, "Alas, Poor Yorick!" *Harper's*, CLIX (1929) , 58; Albert Jay Nock, "The Difficulty of Thinking," *American Mercury*, XLII (1937) , 363.

[11]Nock, *Memoirs*, p. 152.

of the state itself. He believed that all states were merely devices for taking money from one person and giving it to another. According to him they were simply all-powerful agencies available for one economic group to use against another. He saw nothing extraordinary in the American situation.

From just before World War I when he began to publish under his own name until the last ten years of his life, he had been an anarchist. Then, however, Ralph Adams Cram convinced him of the unchanging, brutal nature of man, and he dropped his devotion to pure anarchism.[12] He had always believed that men need societal institutions to develop their sense of intellect, beauty, and morals. He did not change his belief that neither the government nor the state should provide these opportunities for personal growth. He came to concede, however, as Spencer held, that the government should maintain the national defense, secure citizens against trespasses on their property and person, enforce obligation of contract, and make justice costless and easily accessible. Before that time he would have been pleased if the state had passed away.

Elites in the State

In most of his writings he put his trust in men, not procedures and rules. Nock's position clearly concurred with that of Babbitt, and they both thought that America needed an elite. This elite could make any social system work, and its absence would cause even the best social structure to collapse.

Both stated that the American Remnant had been discarded in favor of a ruling class with one standard for admission: money. Nock said that American capitalists had turned the whole of national history into "a ruthless rampage of the instinct

---

[12]Nock, *ibid.*, pp. 136 ff., 206, 331 ff. Nock, *Journal of Forgotten Days*, pp. 105 ff. Albert Jay Nock, "A Little Conserva-tive," *Atlantic Monthly*, CLVIII (1936), 484.

for expansion upon a vast field of exploitable richness."[13]
Deploring the quality of the ruling class, he commented that it
was primarily concerned with gaining personal wealth. Men
with such ideals either cannot or will not turn the energies of
the nation towards civilization. Agreeing with his acquaintance
Lincoln Steffens, he said that "Go and get it!" summarized the
advice of America's visible elite to the young.

If the country could rid its upper-class of a middle-class
regard for money, Nock believed it could free itself from its
present mentality. It could then establish colleges and
universities with proper purposes. With such institutions, it
could proceed to develop a critical sense it lacked in all areas
of its culture.

In 1937 Nock stated that instead of relying upon the
intelligent and educated Remnant, America tossed it onto the
rubbish heap while "the stupidest millionaire in sight," Franklin
Roosevelt, marched into the White House "to the accompani-
ment of a deafening fanfare of adulation for his almost
superhuman abilities."[14] Nock not only denounced Franklin
Roosevelt, he also called leaders of such disparate wealth and
social conscience as Henry Ford and Herbert Hoover symbols
of a misdirected society. Such people were "dreadful swine"
and represented in his mind the forces of "ignorance, brutality,
and indecency."[15] Men of no refinement had such a hold upon
America that no person of culture could find a meaningful
place in the social structure. In Nock's view, which was
probably correct, the nation considered the Remnant
superfluous.

With his own alienation from society, he could speak from
experience. During the 1930's and afterwards, he associated

---

[13]Nock, *Free Speech,* p. 42.

[14]Nock, *ibid.,* p. 137.

[15]Albert Jay Nock, "On the Practice of Smoking in Church," *Harper's,*
CLX (1930), 316. Nock, *Memoirs,* pp. 52-53.

with only a few personal friends. Aside from them, few cared
what Nock thought. The nation was too concerned with
practical matters to worry about any supposed Remnant. The
ruling class in America showed no concern for the Remnant
and did not even envy it. The ruling millionaires had no
measure of individual worth other than the monetary scale.

Social Progress

Like Babbitt, Nock stated that efforts to cope with social
problems through legal actions of the government would fail.
Society as such cannot be improved. Each individual, rather,
must progress before society as a whole can move forward. Nock
therefore ridiculed efforts of professors and other intellectuals
to advise civil government. He condemned the Wisconsin Idea
specifically, for instance, as an "imbecile socio-politico-economic
nostrum" resulting from "inspired idiocy."[16]

Nock claimed that he sweated with agony at the sight of
liberals. They tinkered with the social organism which he
thought had best be left alone. He quoted approvingly the
British conservative Falkland's statement that "when it is not
necessary to change, it is necessary *not* to change."[17] Even the
misery and hunger of the Great Depression did not convince
Nock that the time for change had come.

Attempts at reform result in damage to society at large
because no man can foretell all the factors involved in change.
Some contingency invariably arises which gives a measure a cast
foreign to its original intent. As Nock looked back upon the
history of revolution, for instance, he knew of none including
the American which had not cost more than it had gained.

At heart, Nock felt that the passion for uplift overplayed
the misery of hard circumstances. He did not think that a
utopia would be desirable. Men would soon tire of it. Besides,
he believed that life's rewards come from struggle and challenge.

---

[16]Nock, *Henry George,* p. 200.
[17]Nock, *Memoirs,* pp. 6-7.

People do not mind poverty, anyway, if they are accustomed to nothing better.

He dismissed the attempts by reformers to suggest new ideas and modes of living to the Masses. He did not think they would be able to assimilate them. He urged his contemporaries like Brand Whitlock not to forget that time is an important factor in social change, for the Masses cling to traditional social patterns. Indeed, he warned, if Mass-man is Neanderthalic rather than human, the Masses would never willingly support a humane civilization.

An ambivalence characterized all Nock's thought on the advisability of working for social progress. On one hand, he flatly stated:

> *There is no social engineering that can radically renovate a civilization and change its character, and at the same time keep it going, for civilization is an affair of the human spirit, and the direction of the human spirit cannot be reset by means that are, after all, mechanical. The best thing is to follow the order of nature, and let a moribund civilization simply rot away, and indulge what hope one can that it will be followed by one that is better.*[18]

Yet he thought that individual change was possible. Contact with good books and conversation could transform many crude people into men with a feeling for intellect, beauty, morals, and conduct.[19] If enough people would change, all society would progress. Thus the proper kind of education became central to his social philosophy. He thought that if makers of educational policy would adopt his ideas, chaos could be averted.

In the absence of such education, however, all a wise social philosopher could do, he asserted, was to leave his ideas for

---

[18]Nock, *Journal of Forgotten Days*, p. 117.

[19]Nock, *Memoirs*, p. 47. Albert J. Nock, "Culture Migrates to the U.S.A.," *American Mercury*, XLVI (1939), 481 ff.

men to consider as they passed down the road to destruction. With Mass-man in control of society, Nock did not expect many of his ideas to be accepted, for the Masses could not desire the regeneration of society. In his opinion, they only wanted operational knowledge to increase the material abundance of the life they already had. Although Nock saw many educated and intelligent men in America, he agreed with Henry Adams that they were outcasts in a country which primarily honored the production, distribution, and acquisition of wealth.

HIGHER EDUCATION: THE GENERATION OF THE REMNANT

Consistent with his views on social change, Nock denounced higher education for operational utility. He considered professorial involvement in the political scene mischievous and a nonclassical curriculum destructive of true education. He did not specifically condemn research as such, but it most certainly did not figure in his plans for higher education. He thought that the faculty of a college should devote all its energies to the development of the students' character. He vigorously opposed collegiate involvement in the world of affairs. Since the Masses control America, they would mischievously use the advice offered by the professoriate because they would direct it toward ends not beneficial for the welfare of society. Changes in the curriculum of colleges and universities themselves were creating the illusion of educating people when the kind of education really needed was in fact not taking place. Of crucial significance in Nock's thought, as in Babbitt's, was the idea that the new curriculum was making the creation of the American Remnant practically impossible. This situation drew most of Nock's attention when he wrote about educational affairs, for he felt that it spelled utter doom for the future of civilization in the United States.

The Bane of Culture: The Popular Notion of Equality

Nock feared that the prevailing notion of equality would prevent the Remnant from ever becoming large enough to work as a regenerative force upon the country. The nation had accepted the view that everyone should receive an education because everyone had to possess the operational knowledge to vote intelligently, but Nock did not agree that everyone should vote and hence did not think the rationale for universal education valid. He thought that America should face up to the fact that probably not more than thirty thousand of its people were capable of thinking closely and disinterestedly on any subject. Realizing this, the country should then drop its policy of universal education. If it did not, he warned, it would continue to lower potentially great minds to the level of the mediocre through its system of common schools. He asserted that the nation had equated education and literacy and hence had promoted a universal education resulting in literacy for all and education for none. He called for but could not foresee the development of an educational system with different standards for those of different potential.

Universal education, Nock reiterated, had foundered because "it is condemned to the impossible fantastic task of making silk purses out of sows' ears."[20] Since most students in his opinion were incapable of being educated, he could not see how the schools could escape the necessity of watering down their requirements to something near the "moron standard."[21] How, he asked, could such schools produce the natural elite which the nation so desperately needed if it were to become a viable culture?

---

[20]Nock, *Memoirs*, p. 261.

[21]Nock, *Book of Journeyman*, p. 19.

He concluded that America would have to drop its fears of favoring one class at the expense of others. It should oppose the popular resentment which labeled discrimination in education as undemocratic and follow his view of the precepts of Thomas Jefferson.[22] Nock, a serious student of Jefferson, heartily approved of Jefferson's plan for a limited educational enrollment. It provided that everyone should attend primary school but that only the best ten from each primary school should advance to secondary school, the best ten from there should go to college, and the best ten from each college should study at the university. Nock, like Jefferson, thought that his process would establish the Remnant by annually raking the natural elite of intelligence and wisdom "from the rubbish."[23]

When he wrote these lines, not less than one percent as he desired but more than twelve percent of the young people between the ages of eighteen and twenty-one were enrolled in college. Nock thought that large numbers of students were preventing teachers from giving proper time to each educable one. Estimating that ninety percent of the college students were uneducable, he suggested that the average collegian, a "ruinous nuisance," should best be hoeing corn and his "half-witted flapper desk mate" cleaning house.[24] Perhaps the professoriate would then regain its interest in instruction and turn from its concern for position and money. Until colleges and universities admit only the few with natural ability, Nock did not see how they could concentrate on fulfilling their proper function of developing the American Remnant.

---

[22]Nock, *Theory of Education,* p. 33.

[23]Albert Jay Nock, "The Absurdity of Teaching English," *Bookman,* LXIX (1929), 118.

[24]Nock, *loc. cit.*

Formative and Instrumental Knowledge

Nock did not think that the preparation of the Remnant had anything to do with developing the operational utility of the Masses. He called the former education and the latter training. In Nock's opinion, the differences between education and training were so great that they had little to do with one another. Education, he asserted, involved what he called formative knowledge. Training, on the other hand, entailed education for operational utility or, as he called it, instrumental knowledge. The distinction between education and training might briefly be stated as the same as that between being and doing. The one involves what a person is and the other concerns what he does.[25]

Formative knowledge, Nock illustrated, produces an Emerson, while instrumental knowledge produces an Edison. Nock placed a creative genius like Edison in the same category as an electrical repairman. In his opinion both were technicians and knew how to make operational use of knowledge. Both lacked the sense of beauty, disinterestedness, and humanity characteristic of a cultured man like Emerson.

Nock admitted the need for Edisons and wanted institutes established for their training. He did not want education for operational utility, however, to prevent colleges from introducing the natural elite to formative knowledge.[26] He did not even want any school which dealt with instrumental knowledge to be called a college or a university. These terms implied education, and in his opinion instrumental knowledge had nothing to do with education. It was training.[27]

He believed that after the breakdown of the classical college, American colleges and universities had turned from

---

[25]Nock, *Memoirs*, pp. 269-270; Nock, *Free Speech*, p. 216.

[26]Nock, *Theory of Education*, p. 141.

[27]Nock, *ibid.*, p. 116.

formative knowledge to training. In 1932 he stated that their attention to professional and scientific studies made it impossible to receive an education in any college or university in the country. Nock did not object to professional and scientific studies, but he decried their intrusion into institutions which he maintained should serve as agents for the creation of the American Remnant.

He admitted that he knew of no rational answer why the Remnant could not be educated in the same institutions which also trained the Masses in the techniques necessary for getting along in the world of affairs. He merely observed that in fact they could not. In his opinion, these institutions inevitably neglected formative education and focused on operative knowledge. With the general population honoring material gain as it did, all the students apparently became interested in making money. In such an atmosphere, even the educable lose the will to develop their intellects and character and, instead, rush into the acquisition of knowledge which will enable them to operate more effectively on the American political, social, and economic scene.[28]

I do not mean to imply that the work of the training-school is bad. . . . I mean only that it is in all respects so different from the work of an educational institution that the attempt to compass both under the same general direction is bound to be ineffectual, and that the mere force of volume would always tend to drive the latter out.[29]

He specifically attacked the inclusion of instrumental knowledge in the curriculum:

Instrumental knowledge, knowledge of the sort which bears directly on doing something or getting something, should have no place there [in the school or college].[30]

---

[28]Nock, *ibid.*, pp. 122 ff.
[29]Nock, *ibid.*, pp. 140-141.
[30]Nock, *ibid.*, p. 50.

In all his writings, Nock did not consider where instrumental training should take place. He assumed that training for the Masses would increase their operational efficiency, and he wanted nothing to do with it. His only concern lay in the formative education which would assist in the creation of the Remnant. This education was of the most crucial importance for the elite which was to rule society.

He knew that formative knowledge was not useful in an operational sense, and he defended it accordingly.

It was easy to say that the earlier discipline is mediaeval and out of relation to modern life, for in a sense that is true; but it is true in a sense easily misunderstood and distorted. It was easy to say that this discipline sends out its votaries quite unprepared to meet the actual conditions of present-day living, for that also is true in a sense; it did not send them out with any direct, specific preparation for getting anything or for doing anything. This it never did, never pretended to do. A general preparation it did give an educable person, first by inculcating habits of orderly, profound, and disinterested thought; and second, by giving him an immense amount of experienced acquaintance with the way the human mind had worked in all departments of its activity.[31]

The college curriculum devoted to formative knowledge which Nock devised obviously had little to do with the operational world. It included Greek and Latin literature, mathematics through differential calculus, six or eight weeks of formal logic, and a class in the history of the English language. That was all. The four-year collegiate course would consist of nothing else. Nock would have allowed no elective subjects in his curriculum because he thought they would merely confuse the student. Social sciences and modern languages possessed possible operational utility; so he ruled them out of his curriculum. Neither would he admit any scientific study, since he likewise

---

[31]Nock, *ibid.*, pp. 66-67.

believed that science was instrumental, not formative, knowledge.[32] He never pretended to understand science and could not imagine that it could help man to lead a more humane life.

Nock loved classical studies. Like Babbitt, he valued Greek and Latin because of their disciplinary value. Of more importance, however, he maintained that since Greek and Roman literature are the longest and most continuous records available to modern man, they reflect the views on life of civilizations which had matured. They, therefore, according to him, lead to maturity and hence are formative.[33] Making up the greatest tradition available to the twentieth century, they provide the student with the material for acquiring the characteristics of the Remnant. Nock thought that this Great Tradition, as he called the classics, possessed the generative power to save modern civilization. Without it, society would "lapse into decay and death."[34]

Unfortunately, he lamented, science and the elective system, combined with vocational education, had effectively destroyed the study of the Great Tradition. He could not foresee American colleges and universities returning to it. As he viewed the recent history of American higher education, he concluded that in spite of all their changes, colleges and universities were producing a poorer graduate than ever before. All their grand buildings and elaborate curricular schemes were of no avail because they were failing to educate their students. He could not see how great men could arise in America until the distinction between formative and instrumental knowledge became implicit in the practice and technique of collegiate teaching. By putting the educable youth "in the way of right thinking, clear thinking, mature and profound thinking," American colleges

---

[32]Albert Jay Nock, "The Value to the Clergyman of Training in the Classics," *School Review*, XVI (1908), 385.

[33]Nock, *Theory of Education*, pp. 51-53.

[34]Nock, *ibid.*, p. 157.

and universities could become agents of culture.[35] Instead, by neglecting mature studies, they were dooming America to perpetual adolescence.

With his estimation of the mental ability of the general population, Nock considered as wasted time the efforts of educators to raise the intelligence of the public. Even if the state were to allow any real education to take place, the Neanderthalic Masses would be unable to react to it. Direct efforts to overcome mass ignorance would always result in failure, he prophesied, because modern man did not possess the requisite mental capacity.

He asserted that colleges and universities, moreover, could never offer much hope of changing anyone from established social patterns because of the nature of the modern state. He was convinced that the state was using education to synthesize a devotion to it and its rulers. Along with all the other social institutions such as the press and the pulpit, colleges and universities could only maintain and confirm the dominant social structure.

The healthy college-bred half-wit, male and female, makes the best kind of serf-minded adult. We have turned them out in shoals for thirty-five years, and their spirit rules the country.[36]

A system producing such people has little to do with developing men of wisdom and refinement. Nock could not conceive of the state, coercive and exploitive as it is by nature, being expected to do anything else. Those in control of it would not allow colleges and universities to produce men who would dislodge them from their positions of power.

---

[35]Nock, *ibid.,* p. 124.

[36]Nock, *Journal of Forgotten Days,* p. 7.

Despair

Nock's opposition to higher education for operational utility follows naturally enough from his views of man and society. If most men were Neanderthalic, they certainly could not be turned into the Remnant simply by enduring four years of college. After the rise to power of the common man and the decline of the old aristocracy in America during the nineteenth century, Nock could reasonably argue that the Masses would indeed not tolerate a form of education of no use to them and hence had destroyed the classical college as the standard for higher education.

Because of the passing of the educational pattern which he cherished, Nock could explain his own alienation from American society. Few places in the country offered men the education necessary for the creation of the Remnant of which he was a part. Instead of graduates of literary refinement, he saw graduates prepared to cope with the complexities of industrial America. These men seemed to lack an appreciation for the standards which Nock valued, and if Nock were to maintain his own sense of esteem, he had to lament the failure of the new industrial leadership to sympathize with the culture he represented. Like Henry Adams, he felt estranged from the America of the dynamo and regretted the passing of the humanistic ideals he knew.

The formalistic higher education which he idealized bore little relation to the industrial complex about him, and he did not bother to discuss whether indeed some accommodation between formative and instrumental knowledge might not be possible. Yet, if society were not to abandon technology, some accommodation had to be made. Instead of simply stating that instrumental knowledge within a college would destroy students' interest in formative knowledge, he should have discussed in detail the best positions of both in an educational scheme. This he refused to do. He simply called contemporary educational

and social practices materialistic and subversive of formative
ideals. In renouncing the present in this fashion, Nock admitted the truly reactionary nature of his views. He longed for a
return to the past.

Perhaps the sociopolitical past which Nock envisioned had
to a degree existed at one time. During the early decades of the
Republic, men like Washington, the two Adamses, Jefferson,
Madison, and Monroe represented to a great extent the kind of
leadership Nock recommended. A rather small, visible elite,
generally well-read and literate, they approximated the Remnant described by Nock. They received both the political and
social support and deference of a general population in some
regards similar to Nock's Masses.

Attributing the nature of the sociopolitical leadership to
peculiarities in the formal higher education of the day is not
justified. Too many factors other than college curricula come
into play in the life of a nation. Furthermore, Nock himself
realized that cultivated, wise men of character existed in
twentieth-century American life. No evidence exists for his
belief that the classical college produced more graduates conforming to his notion of the Remnant than the modern
university.

Students in eighteenth-century America were probably no
more refined or humane than students in the twentieth century.
Nock was correct in much of his criticism of the contemporary
American college. Histories of American colleges and universities readily reveal that too many students disdained academic
life and looked upon college mainly as a chance for having a
good time, meeting the right people, picking up proper skills
for desired social groups, and learning the right gambits for
getting ahead.[37] Nock was right to condemn an educational
system which allowed this sort of situation to exist. On the

---

[37]See, for instance, W. H. Cowley, "Overview," pp. 294 ff. and Rudolph,
American College and University, p. 454.

other hand, an examination of the eighteenth- and nineteenth-century classical college fails to reveal a pattern essentially different. Colonial colleges prepared students for positions of status in society. Their students did not appear any more refined than those of modern times. The earlier American students may not have swallowed goldfish or worn coonskin coats, but when Ezra Stiles became President of Yale in 1777, he called them "a bundle of Wild Fire not easily controlled and governed." Students "were wont to express their displeasure with their tutors by stoning their windows or attacking them with clubs if they chanced out after dark."[38] Such traits do not resemble the characteristics of Nock's Remnant. Apparently the Great Tradition was not creating Nock's desired social climate even in the classical college.

In spite of his naiveté, Nock presents a somewhat perplexing problem to the present-day observer. Admittedly his apparent callousness toward those not blessed with great intellectual potential would distress the sensitive. His narrowness in defining the curriculum for colleges and universities would likewise evoke little sympathy among most groups of modern humanists. Treating the general population as rubbish or refusing it the opportunity to become literate reflects an unacceptable moral obtuseness. Yet his critique of American society and education is somewhat disquieting. His analysis may be confused, and his solutions may be repulsive; but the cultivated, refined standards of his Remnant are desperately needed in an age buffeted by a crude, semiliterate mass culture. True, high culture is flourishing in modern America, but what person of taste and judgment cannot become disturbed by the tone of popular culture? Neanderthalic, not cultivated, tastes characterize too much of it.

Nock is a curious conservative in simultaneously repudiating both the masses and the visible elite. If he had castigated

---

[38]Cowley, "Overview," p. 207.

the dominant materialistic values of the middle class and had not also held the masses in contempt, he might have appeared more attractive to critics of the ruling groups of his day. On the other hand, if he had simply bemoaned the low level of mass democracy, he might have gained a hearing from men like those in the Liberty League. In writing disparagingly of both groups, however, he lost the ear of both.

Because he refused to accommodate himself to the social and intellectual patterns of his age, his ideas did not receive wide approval. His major essay dealing with education, *The Theory of Education in the United States,* attracted little comment when it appeared in 1932. Abraham Flexner reviewed it favorably in the *Nation,* but he could not agree with Nock's specific proposals. In another review in the *New Republic,* John Dewey acknowledged Nock's erudition but accurately doubted that the book would find an audience.[39] College and university presidents publicly ignored the book, and apparently no educational institution in the country changed its policy because of Nock. No public arose to purchase the book in large quantities, and it aroused little controversy. Nock correctly appraised his status when he declared himself superfluous. His ideas were too far removed from contemporary conditions to appear relevant to the makers of social and educational policy.

In modern America, higher education had to meet the operational needs of an industrial, democratic society. The confusing array of colleges and universities may have lacked the cultural basis Nock desired, but they satisfied the groups looking for people trained in the skills to keep the country going. Since these groups supplied the finances for higher

---

[39]Abraham Flexner, "Education in America," *Nation,* Feb. 17, 1932, pp. 207-208; John Dewey, "Bending the Twig," *New Republic,* April 13, 1932, pp. 242-244.

education, little opportunity existed for the implementation of Nock's ideas.

Nock did not worry about turning his ideas into reality. He admitted his lack of practical knowledge and dismissed it with the assertion that any deliberate change which would occur in society or education would be mechanical. And he did not consider himself a mechanic. He held no hope that his efforts could lead anywhere. He was, he said, merely voicing an aspiration, a "reverence to a distant, high and unapproachable ideal."[40]

---

[40]Nock, *Theory of Education*, p. 154.

CHAPTER FIVE

ABRAHAM FLEXNER:
Research Universities for America

*The university should by precept and by example en-
deavor to convince the public that in the long run it will
suffer, not gain, if it treats its universities largely as
service institutions.*

ABRAHAM FLEXNER, 1930

ALTHOUGH BOTH BABBITT AND NOCK wished to
return the focus of American colleges and universities toward
character, opposition to higher education for operational utility
could be based upon other wishes. The revolution in American
higher education during the late nineteenth century generally
took the form of educational operational utility. The Germanic
emphasis upon research was one of the main elements in the
revolution, and in Germany, university research did not relate
to societal needs in the same operational sense as it often did
in America. Concern with the development of new breeds of
potatoes, for instance, would have been below the dignity of a
German professor. The Germanic notion of research had little
relationship to the practices of higher education for operational
utility in America.

Men like Daniel Coit Gilman of Johns Hopkins University
and G. Stanley Hall of Clark University envisioned research
universities of a different variety from that developed at the
University of Wisconsin. Conceptual research, unrelated to the

immediate problems of society, held their interest. Although the greater part of the research in American colleges and universities probably related to matters of operational utility, undoubtedly much research did not. Within many American universities the advocates of nonutilitarian research looked condescendingly upon those conducting research of operational utility, and they even implied that their own studies were somehow purer than those of practical value. Harkening back to the Greek disdain of manual work, in some cases they even stated that all factual research is of a lower nature than research of a strictly rational nature. Direct practical research was the least prestigious of all.

This intellectual position is of a radically different nature from those represented by Babbitt and Nock. While men like Babbitt and Nock were calling for more attention to undergraduate instruction, people in the tradition of Gilman and Hall urged more attention to conceptual research. All of them opposed the practices of higher education for operational utility, but they did so for different and conflicting reasons. Babbitt and Nock were basically reactionary in wishing a return to classical concerns, but the advocates of conceptual research opposed the revolution in higher education because they felt it had taken a wrong turn.

A good example of this kind of thinking is to be found in the writings of Abraham Flexner. In contrast to Babbitt and Nock, Flexner did not worry primarily about the effect which the ideal of higher education for operational utility was exercising upon general education and the development of the Remnant. Instead of idolizing the nineteenth-century literary college as they did, he rejected the concept of the classical curriculum. Where Babbitt had abhorred the research orientatation of the German university, he admired it. He criticized American colleges and universities mainly because in functioning in accord with the precepts of operational utility, they were neglecting research of no immediate value. He believed that higher education should be wholly devoted to the advancement of knowledge through nonutilitarian research. Teaching should become a function of a college or university only as it contributes to that end. Thus he opposed higher education for operational utility, but he also depreciated the role of general education.

Objecting to the concept of higher education for operational utility, he believed that it had corrupted the proper function of the university. By relating too closely to the operational needs of society, he asserted, American colleges and universities had lost their devotion to intellectual pursuits. Like Babbitt and Nock, Flexner thought that American colleges and universities had catered too much to materialistic tendencies in American life. His books and articles called for the rejection of strictly vocational courses and extension programs because he said, with some truth, that colleges and universities had set them up in order to make money. He saw no educational value in them. He insisted that institutions of learning had to remain separate from the immediate needs of their social environment if they were to retain their integrity. If the state or society could function more efficiently because of the strictly intellectual efforts of universities, he would be pleased, but the idea of a university setting out to advance anything but knowledge repelled him.

These ideas came almost intact from Gilman's ideal for the American university. Flexner had studied at Johns Hopkins University between 1884 and 1886 when Gilman was attempting to establish the first American research-oriented university. Although Johns Hopkins University had adopted an undergraduate program, Gilman had opposed it. He had wanted a graduate university without an undergraduate college, and he advised his faculty to devote its attention solely to the advancement of knowledge. Flexner later admitted that Gilman's educational standards set the direction for all his own later educational thinking and influenced him in everything he did in his subsequent career in education.[1]

He had come to Johns Hopkins University from his home in Louisville, Kentucky. His parents, Jewish immigrants from Central Europe, were poor, but they instilled in him a desire to do good work. Thus when he received the opportunity to study at Johns Hopkins, which at the time had the highest reputation for scholarship in the country, Flexner went there and made an outstanding record. He studied classics for only two years before he was able to pass the examination which allowed him to graduate.

Together with this quick completion of a collegiate career, Flexner's later experience convinced him that schools, colleges, and universities could accomplish more if they would eliminate needless repetition and stimulate the desire of students to work. After returning to Louisville in 1886, he taught for a brief time in the local high school. Then, responding to a need for private tutoring to prepare wealthy but unruly boys for Eastern colleges, he founded his own preparatory school. He discovered in his school that he was able to prepare his students for successful work in the best colleges after brief periods of instruction.

In fact, his former students performed so well that Charles W. Eliot noticed him. He asked Flexner to write an article describing his methods. The article appeared in the *Atlantic Monthly* in the year 1904 under the title "The Preparatory School."[2]

Writing the article apparently convinced Flexner that he needed more academic training. In 1905-1906 he enrolled at Harvard, where studies awakened his interest in comparative education. He decided to spend the following year abroad. Since his concept of Gilman's university ideals related closely to

---

[1]Abraham Flexner, *I Remember: the Autobiography of Abraham Flexner* (New York, 1940), p. 400.

[2]Abraham Flexner, "The Preparatory School," *Atlantic Monthly*, XCIV (1904), 368-377.

German practices, he went to the University of Berlin. His year there firmly convinced him that German universities were the best in the world.

Upon his return to the United States, Flexner wrote a critique of American higher education entitled *The American College*. Written from the viewpoint of a preparatory school administrator, the book called for more attention to intellectual matters within the college and less to extracurricular affairs.

This book, published in 1908, proved decisive in Flexner's career, for it caught the attention of Henry S. Pritchett, head of the Carnegie Corporation. At the time, the Corporation was about to initiate a major study of medical education in the United States and Canada. On the basis of the book's quality, Pritchett chose Flexner to make the study. The report appeared after two years of extensive research. Flexner had visited every one of the one hundred fifty-five American and Canadian medical schools and described them in detail. The findings were shocking. The facilities of some of their teaching hospitals were so antiquated and unsanitary that he called them death traps. Flexner had discovered that most medical schools were not training the nation's future physicians in even the fundamentals of modern medicine. Too many of them were proprietary institutions existing solely for the profit of their owners. Unscrupulous physicians were operating without any concern for the public welfare. Students who had not even graduated from high school could readily find admission to a medical school, and after their matriculation the curriculum would not prepare them to practice medicine. Even schools sponsored by reputable universities lacked the rudiments of adequate clinical facilities so critical in the education of medical doctors. Flexner recommended that one hundred twenty medical schools be closed.[3]

---

[3]For further details see Abraham Flexner, *Medical Education in the United States and Canada,* Bulletin Number Four of the Carnegie Foundation for the Advancement of Teaching (New York, 1910) ; and Flexner, *I Remember,* pp. 113 ff.

This report made the front pages of the newspapers and brought Flexner a national reputation as an authority on higher education which he enjoyed the rest of his life. Largely as a result of this work, in 1913 John D. Rockefeller, Jr. asked Flexner to join the permanent staff of the General Education Board. For fifteen years Flexner worked for the Board as assistant secretary, secretary, and finally as head of its Division of Studies and Medical Education. The Board, established in 1903 by the Rockefellers, was attempting to raise the level of education throughout the United States. It not only made direct financial grants to educational institutions, but it also tried to improve social and economic conditions in under-developed areas of the country. Its policy assumed that prosperous people would support a better school system than poor people would. For example, the Board sponsored a project to eradicate hookworm in the southeastern United States. It assumed that good health standards would help the people of the area to produce more economically and hence be able to build decent schools.

Flexner's many years with the Board did not change his basic views about American higher education. Upon retiring from it in 1928, he delivered the Rhodes Trust Memorial Lectures at Oxford in which he proposed that American higher education be remodeled along the lines advocated by Gilman at Johns Hopkins a half century earlier. The three lectures, published in 1930 in revised form under the title *Universities— American, English, German,* stressed the superiority of German universities over both the American and the English. Flexner attacked the ideal and practices of higher education for operational utility and called for a complete change in American colleges and universities. He wanted the formulation and transmission of conceptual knowledge to replace all the other phases of university life.

SOCIAL RESPONSIBILITIES OF COLLEGE AND UNIVERSITIES

Flexner maintained that the solution to the complexities of the modern world depend upon intelligence and the devotion with which specialized intellectual functions are discharged. As he looked about him, he observed that the basic assumptions and knowledge held by the population were more or less obsolete. Flexner wanted the country to adapt high level conceptual research to its problems. Like Babbitt and Nock, he believed in the existence of a natural elite and held that only this elite could lead the nation forward. In contrast to Babbitt and Nock, he thought that the characteristics of this elite consisted in its possession not of character but of advanced knowledge. Hence he called for the general population to pay proper respect to the advice of the aristocracy of genius, talent, and training: those who were great scholars and had discovered new concepts basic to knowledge. In this manner society as a whole could keep in pace with the best thought of mankind.

With the accelerated rate of social change, he felt that plans had to be created to cope with social problems. He contrasted the modern world to that of the early nineteenth century as one of increased organization, requiring technical and professional training and experience. Therefore he thought that modern, industrial, urban society depends upon intelligence in specialized fields. Only the advancement of knowledge, in his opinion, could enable modern society to develop that intelligence. Since he thought that only the natural elite possessed the ability to deal with these problems, he held that the failure of colleges and universities to train the elite was leading to a lower quality of life in America. In his opinion, higher education for operational utility was neglecting the creation of the new ideas basic to knowledge and hence could only result in a static society. New concepts on an esoteric, nonoperative level were necessary for a dynamic society.

Only through research-oriented universities, asserted Flexner, could society be lifted from mediocre standards to those of excellence. By developing concepts and by analyzing both experimental data and experience drawn from the actual world, the research scholar could make sense out of the world. In this fashion, scholars could contribute rational constructs to the world at large enabling everyone to understand better the basic nature of reality. In considering the situation of American society, Flexner believed that it needed centers of advanced learning. Without basic research, no society could move forward. Flexner saw no means other than high-level teaching and research for a society to utilize if it wanted to move forward and provide a better life for all. It had to support the advancement of knowledge if it did not want to stagnate.[4]

Flexner stated that the university assumes a key role in a nation's striving to improve itself because it has the task of maintaining and advancing knowledge. He thought that a university could promote the welfare of the nation by focusing upon four major goals: (1) the conservation of knowledge and ideas, (2) the interpretation of knowledge and ideas, (3) the search for truth, and (4) the training of students who will appreciate knowledge and become the scholars of tomorrow.[5] Clearly, he was not concerned with Babbitt's cultural standards or Nock's formative knowledge. He wanted only the development of an intellectual community which would originate new ideas which might act as leavening agents in society. By concentrating on conceptual research, Flexner maintained, American colleges and universities would supply the knowledge necessary for the creation of the ideal society and thus completely satisfy its social responsibility.

---

[4]Abraham Flexner, "Aristocratic and Democratic Education," *Atlantic Monthly*, CVIII (1911), 386 ff.

[5]Abraham Flexner, *Universities—American, English, German*, p. 6.

As he observed modern American universities oriented toward operational utility, he wrote that they largely had deserted their proper intellectual pursuits. Instead of limiting themselves to the conservation, interpretation, and investigation of truth, colleges and universities had assimilated too many activities irrelevant and inconsistent with their true function. He condemned the emphasis on student government, parties, and athletics which provided the student with techniques for operating smoothly in interpersonal situations. He disliked the direct service which professors and educational institutions were rendering to enhance the operational efficiency of society. A college or university, he stated, should not let any rationalization turn it from its concern for activities of a predominantly intellectual character.

> *Universities have become bigger, richer, and more hectic. The best of them have at many points risen to their new opportunities and obligations. But simultaneously they have at other points sunk to depths at which Eliot and Gilman would have been horrified. So rapid has been their expansion that they have not taken time to survey critically many of the new activities which they have so lightly taken on. Once committed, they have justified their absurdities by mere words— —"service," "democracy," or some other label that merely covers a running sore.*[6]

Believing that actual participation of colleges and universities in political and social affairs would degrade their intellectual nature, he called upon them to refrain from it. He did not think that any service they could render through such direct activities would compensate for the harm done to their academic work.

---

[6]Abraham Flexner, "The University in American Life," *Atlantic Monthly,* CXLIX (1932), 621.

Professorial Involvement in Practical Matters

The social sciences must be detached from the conduct of business, the conduct of politics, the reform of this, that, and the other, if they are to develop as sciences, even though they continuously need contact with the phenomena of business, the phenomena of politics, the phenomena of social experimentation.[7]

To a certain extent, contacts between faculty and business . . . are essential to the faculty itself. To that extent—and to that extent only—such contacts should take place. But as the function of the university is the increase of knowledge and the training of men, contacts and responsibilities are harmful to the university, and hence to society, as soon as they multiply beyond the point I have indicated.[8]

Flexner never wavered from his conviction that the involvement of faculty members in practical affairs would harm the professors' scholarly pursuits. He would not have approved of faculty members holding advisory or staff positions like those the professors in Wisconsin held. He even doubted whether academic men should serve on advisory councils, for he questioned whether they could discharge their advisory responsibilities without distorting their scholarship.[9] He doubted whether anyone, even under the best circumstances, could really look objectively at social, political, and economic issues, and he feared that involvement in the world of affairs would make objective scholarship all the more difficult. Partisanship, with all the emotional stresses which inevitably arise, would seriously affect

---

[7]Flexner, *Universities,* p. 17.

[8]Flexner, *ibid.,* pp. 148-149.

[9]Flexner, *ibid.,* pp. 15-16; Abraham Flexner, "Address," American Philosophical Society, *Proceedings,* LXIX (1930), 263.

nearly anyone's rational perspective. Moreover, the time spent with such activities would not bring an appropriate return to intellectual work.[10]

Essentially, Flexner thought that professors should observe society but not assume responsibilities for it. He wondered, however, whether the line between the academy and its environment could be maintained. He doubted whether faculty members could study matters with practical implications without feeling impelled to advise governmental officials about the conclusions. Furthermore, he did not see how the advance of knowledge could be effectively championed if scholars allowed societal needs to set the course of their investigations.

He thought that colleges and universities should limit their responsibilities to educating students in scholarly pursuits and to investigating topics of scholarly significance.[11] They eventually would make their outstanding contribution to society not in increasing its operating efficiency by becoming research agencies for nonacademic bodies or sources of experts to solve specific problems, but in providing the concepts fundamental to man's progressive understanding of himself and his world. Operational techniques themselves rest upon conceptual knowledge. Flexner feared that a rather complete concern with the former would prevent the advance of the latter. Eventually, operational knowledge could not progress beyond the limits of man's basic conceptual knowledge. Hence the use of professors in solving problems of an operational nature appeared short-sighted to Flexner. Referring to the direct response of colleges and universities to the immediate needs of their society environments, he stated, "Service [has almost] destroyed the very conception of the university as an institution of learning."[12] He

---

[10]Flexner, *Universities,* p. 10.

[11]Flexner, *Universities,* p. 132.

[12]Flexner, *Universities,* p. 339.

wanted the university to be an ivory tower, a haven in which scholars could advance conceptual knowledge, not solve the functional problems of the world. The ideas which they produced would be the contribution of higher education to American society.

The university will make its outstanding contribution to human thought and, in the long run, to human society if it assists men to comprehend.[13]

Flexner admitted that educational institutions outside colleges and universities would have to deal with operational matters as they did in Germany, but he did not develop his views about them in detail. His attention focused upon the failure of American colleges and universities to function in accord with his purpose for higher education.

He feared that professors often turned from investigation of conceptual problems to those of practical value because of their need for money. Similarly, he thought that American colleges and universities themselves had become institutions of operational utility for financial rewards. State universities felt that service would bring them more money from legislatures, and private universities felt that it would induce larger donations from alumni, business corporations, and philanthropic foundations.[14]

American universities . . . go into the market place and do a thriving business with the mob. They advertise their shoddy wares in newspapers and periodicals. . . . Many of the activities carried on by numerous universities are little short of dishonest; but the business goes on, because it pays—for that and for no other reason.[15]

---

[13]Abraham Flexner, "Failings of Our Graduate Schools," *Atlantic Monthly*, CXLIX (1932), p. 449.

[14]Flexner, *ibid.*, p. 130.

[15]Flexner, "University in American Life," p. 626.

University Extension

Flexner condemned extension and correspondence courses as outstanding examples of the corruption of American higher education. He thought they had all but destroyed the focus of the university upon intellectual affairs.[16] Flexner admitted that extension and correspondence courses could possibly be substantial, the students competent, and the instruction of high quality. In theory, Flexner saw nothing wrong with them. In practice, however, he said that their concern for subjects unrelated to the advancement of knowledge detracted from the intellectual orientation of the university. In sponsoring courses dealing with matters like the techniques of potato growing, American universities were diverting scholars from attending to their proper concern: the pursuit of conceptual knowledge. He did not think that correspondence courses contributed to the serious study of business, society, or economics, but rather furnished practical men such as advertisers and salesmen with the tricks of their trades. In his opinion, they represented a plague upon learning.[17]

INTELLECTUAL STANDARDS AND EDUCATIONAL RESPONSIBILITIES

Flexner's position differed from that of Babbitt and that of Nock because of his insistence that the university should instill in students the notion that "service is the keynote of modern social life."[18] Babbitt and Nock had both deplored collegiate service to society. Flexner, on the other hand, reasoned that students who studied with professors who were investigating basic issues of society would be likely themselves to form new

---

[16]Flexner, *Universities,* p. 339.

[17]Flexner, *ibid.,* pp. 130 ff., 165.

[18]Abraham Flexner, *A Modern College and a Modern School* (New York, 1923), pp. xv-xvi.

views of society. These views could easily lead the students to social service because they would find the existing social order offensive. Flexner's ideas, of course, contrasted sharply with the rationale of higher education for operational utility because he wanted service to come as a by-product, not as a purpose, of colleges and universities.[19] By training good students, colleges and universities devoted to basic research would make far more of a practical impact on society than those oriented to operating techniques.

Revealing the fundamentally progressive nature of his position, he stated that proper education in a democracy equips the individual "to exercise his powers in helping to determine the precise form the social revolution will next take."[20] He criticized American colleges and universities because he felt they were organized to maintain the social status quo rather than to prepare their students for creative thinking about basic problems. Flexner considered higher education one of the means through which the governing portion of society was endeavoring to perpetuate its beliefs and ideals.[21] Since he thought that the dominant class valued wealth and technical power above all else, he thought that men with distorted values had made the nation's colleges and universities into institutions designed to perpetuate unwise materialistic ideals.

He stated that the whole materialistic bent of American life hampered the educational efforts of the university. For instance, Flexner thought that undergraduates looked upon education as a means of acquiring techniques to raise their social standing. He explained their primary devotion to social and athletic affairs by pointing out that such activities enable students to

---

[19]Abraham Flexner, "Adjusting the College to American Life," *Science*, March 5, 1909, p. 364.

[20]Flexner, "Aristocratic and Democratic Education," p. 390.

[21]Flexner, *ibid.*, p. 386; Abraham Flexner, "A Modern University," *Atlantic Monthly*, CXXXVI (1925), 535.

operate in certain social spheres.[22] Denying that intellectual standards animated the higher education of his day, he asserted that colleges and universities were emphasizing the ability to get ahead in society. They were therefore exercising a harmful, not helpful, influence in the creation of the knowledge requisite for the advancement of American civilization.[23]

In Flexner's view, colleges and universities were catering to fleeting, transient, and immediate demands, placing material objects above ideas.[24] He observed large sums of money flowing into higher education; but instead of being used for the improvement of intellectual functions, it went for elaborate buildings, equipment, or stadia.[25] He adhered to the ideas of Gilman who had put his available financial resources at Johns Hopkins University into men, not buildings. Flexner complained that American colleges and universities find huge sums for athletics, but dig as they might, they could not find enough for professorial salaries. If the American university directed its resources to academic purposes, he asserted, it would have all the money it needed for its legitimate concerns."[26] He did not think this would happen. Not enough people wanted it to.

Flexner further lamented that faculty members did not really value scholarship. If so, he said, they would have eliminated the unnecessary administrative work they perform. He wanted them to curb the irrelevancies and incidentals which overshadowed true educational purposes.

In Flexner's wide travels he found no one who felt the conditions of universities "most favorable to sound thinking

---

[22]Flexner, *Universities*, p. 69.

[23]Flexner, "Failings of Graduate Schools," p. 447.

[24]Flexner, *Universities*, p. 44.

[25]Flexner, "Failings of Graduate Schools," p. 451.

[26]Flexner, *Universities*, p. 204.

and contemplative living."[27]   He did not know exactly what would solve the problems of American higher education as he saw them.   Although he did not take a view as pessimistic as Nock's, he admitted that change in higher education comes exceeding slowly.   He felt that colleges and universities were burdened by so many problems that he could suggest no sure remedies.[28]

He thought that a shift in the functions and structures of American higher education might help.   He wanted undergraduate and graduate study assigned to different institutions. Then, he maintained, both the college and the university could better fulfill their intellectual tasks.   As he viewed the condition of the modern American university, he saw a number of structures included within it: colleges for high school graduates, research institutions, professional schools, extension divisions, correspondence schools, and athletic leagues.   He differed from most university presidents of his day because he decried this situation.   Most of them approved.[29]   He wanted the graduate school of arts and sciences, certain professional schools, and selected research institutions to constitute the major part of the American university.

He declared that the college should exist apart from graduate schools and attempt primarily to train the intellects of the students.   It should prepare its students with the basic factual material which a person needs before he can begin exploring the unknown.   For students entering professional schools, he recommended the development of an undergraduate curriculum related to each professional school.   Through his own 1910 report on medical education in the United States and Canada,

---

[27]Flexner, *I Remember*, p. 363.

[28]Flexner, "University in American Life," p. 620.

[29]See, for example, the articles by B. H. Bode, L. D. Coffman, W. H. Cowley, W. H. Kilpatrick, and H. N. MacCracken in *The Journal of Higher Education*, II (1931).

his position on preprofessional education had given support to
the organization of the premedical curriculum along professional
lines. Modern undergraduate premedical requirements approach the basic pattern which he desired for all preprofessional
education. Since undergraduate teaching would detract from
university professors' research, he opposed the inclusion of
collegiate work into the university.

He called for the establishment of universities composed
only of professors and students actively involved in advancing
knowledge. A small number of graduate students would work
closely with the professors, but research, not teaching and public
service, would set the tone of Flexner's university. He wanted
universities to drop their concern for students' nonintellective
needs and to rebuff the public's demand that they become
" 'service' stations for the general public."[30]   The university
could then become "a free society of students, professors, and
pupils mingling naturally in the pursuit of intellectual aims."[31]
Concern with any other goals would subvert this pursuit, the
raison d'être of American colleges and universities. Thus a
college or university would not give attention to any matter of
operational utility.

The Curriculum

If American higher education were changed structurally,
Flexner thought that colleges and universities could institute a
curriculum which would lead to the fulfillment of their
intellectual goals. In developing his own ideal course of undergraduate study, despite his own training in Greek and Latin, he
rejected the classics as the heart of the curriculum. He saw no
purpose in them for modern society and thought that any
remaining requirements in the classics should be abolished. He

---

[30]Flexner, *Universities*, p. 45.

[31]Flexner, "Modern University," p. 535.

ridiculed as make-believe the argument that mental discipline results from the study of Latin and Greek.[32]

Instead he favored subjects which would lead the student to the boundaries of modern thought and prepare him for research into the unknown. First of all, he desired science because he believed it to be an object of man's curiosity and of benefit to man.[33] Secondly, Flexner held that if the proper study of man is man, every educated person should understand the great works of literature.[34] Together with history, philosophy, and art, these subjects would constitute the proper course of study within the American college and prepare the student for entrance into active research in the university.

Like Babbitt and Nock, he attacked the free elective principle. He insisted that men reach the border of knowledge by studying a few subjects thoroughly, not by skimming over many. He disliked the free elective system under which a student could take almost any course because the system failed to meet the demands of "organic continuity in training."[35] He did not take the same position as Babbitt and Nock, who wanted all students to study exactly the same subjects in college. Flexner favored, rather, a system in which the student could choose one of a number of basic groups of courses. Once the initial choice had been made, the student would be required to take all the courses in his particular group. This limited elective system, corresponding somewhat to majoring in many colleges and universities, was to give the student the continuity and depth which Flexner feared that free election would not provide.

---

[32]Abraham Flexner, "Education as Mental Discipline," *Atlantic Monthly*, CXIX (1917), 456; Abraham Flexner, "The Problem of College Pedagogy," *Atlantic Monthly*, CIII (1909), 841.

[33]Abraham Flexner, *Medical Education: A Comparative Study* (New York, 1925), p. 152.

[34]Abraham Flexner, *Funds and Foundations* (New York, 1952), p. 133.

[35]Abraham Flexner, *The American College* (New York, 1908), p. 97.

Although he did not want practical training to replace training for intellectual research, he did advocate the organization of higher education "to realize the intellectual and cultural values of the practical or professional discipline or activity which will come next."[36] When possible, Flexner maintained, the curriculum should deal with the conceptual bases of the student's future vocation. If a society were to be influenced by conceptual research, the professions should be composed of people able to think creatively. Moreover, such education would attract the student because of his own self-interest.[37] Flexner did not mean to imply that higher education should be concerned with the operating procedures often associated with vocational courses like cooking, carpentry, journalism, and the techniques of teaching. He called for the abolition of such courses.[38] He wanted only studies of a predominantly intellectual nature to characterize American colleges and universities, but he saw no reason why professional training could not be made intellectual by focusing upon the exploration of conceptual problems. Such an education certainly involves "the free, resourceful and unhampered play of intelligence."[39] To the extent that any vocation has a basis in conceptual thought, he felt that it deserves a place in the university.

Although the German pattern of higher education had evolved historically in response to social prestige and traditional prejudices, Flexner thought it had developed because of efforts to separate conceptual thinking from job training. According to him, German education had long maintained the distinction between vocations with an intellectual foundation and those

[36]Flexner, *Modern College and Modern School*, p. 42.

[37]Flexner, "Preparatory School," p. 842.

[38]Abraham Flexner, "The Prepared Mind," *School and Society*, June 26, 1937, pp. 870-871.

[39]Flexner, "Failings of Graduate Schools," p. 448.

demanding merely muscular or mental dexterity. German universities had included only the top-level professions like law and medicine with a basis in conceptual thought. Professions like engineering, supposedly lacking a firm conceptual foundation, had been relegated to technical schools outside the universities. Flexner advocated the adoption of the same pattern for America.

Flexner's realization that culture and vocation should not necessarily be considered separately make his ideas radically different from those of Babbitt and Nock, who saw no connection. All three stressed the necessity for a purely intellectual collegiate experience devoid of preparation in the techniques handy for operational utility, but Flexner denied that the curriculum should be exclusively literary. In fact he asserted that advocates of literary culture were reactionary. Their position, he said, had been valid in nineteenth-century America when men with literary educations could enter almost any profession. The twentieth century with all its complexities, however, had made literary education obsolete. To the arguments of men like Babbitt and Nock, he countered that the classics were naive.[40] He thought that advocates of classical education had too long been hypnotized by the term culture. "A nation's stock of ideas and achievements in art, science, philosophy, manners, industry—this is its culture."[41] All would receive the attention of university scholars if Flexner had attained his goals for higher education.

Higher Education for Research

Flexner wanted to keep higher education simple in both structure and function so scholars could devote their full energies to research. His ideal found realization when two wealthy

---

[40]Flexner, "College Pedagogy," p. 841.

[41]Abraham Flexner, "Purpose in the American College," *School and Society*, Dec. 12, 1925, p. 735.

residents of Baltimore gave him the money to establish the Institute for Advanced Study at Princeton. In 1930 he became its first director, and he held the post until 1939 when he retired. There he appointed to the staff only a few brilliant scholars who could do completely as they wished. At the Institute he had no faculty meetings, no committees, and no organized groups of students. Instead he merely sponsored a group of scholars and some postdoctoral students who cooperated in their efforts to advance knowledge.

Before him as his model he held Gilman's idea of a German university in America modified by the knowledge of the work of his brother, Simon Flexner, who had headed the Rockefeller Institute for Medical Research in New York City at a time when the Institute maintained a staff of renowned research scientists with whom a number of gifted young men worked. Its educational functions were carried on informally, and the Institute offered no degrees.

In developing the Institute for Advanced Study at Princeton, Flexner had to decide whether he would follow the basic design of the German university and include graduate students working toward the Ph.D. He decided against the German example. Instead, he followed the pattern of the Rockefeller Institute. He excluded even doctoral candidates. He wanted only a few great masters, each with a few postdoctoral disciples. In discussing his ideas with leading thinkers and educators around the world, he indicated clearly that he wanted only the most able scholars and that if enough renowned men in an academic discipline could not be obtained, he would not include the discipline in his school. The Princeton Institute opened with three theoretical schools: the School of Mathematics, the School of Economics and Politics, and the School of Humanistic Studies. He planned to keep the number of schools flexible, deleting or adding them as conditions changed.

The scholars who joined the staff of the Institute justified his trust. Including such noted figures as Edward M. Earle,

Albert Einstein, Ernst Herzfeld, David Mitrany, Erwin Panofsky, Winfield W. Riefler, Walter W. Stewart, Oswald Veblen, and Hermann Weyl, the Institute soon gained an international reputation for outstanding scholarship. The Institute has remained small as Flexner envisioned it, for a large number of scholars would hamper the free and untrammeled exchange of ideas which best occurs through the informal means possible only in a small group.

Enjoying a close relationship with Princeton University, the Institute fulfilled Flexner's highest expectations. It has not, however, served as a guide for changing American higher education. His plan was too restricted to satisfy the need for the education of students. A number of havens for scholars to pursue research have developed, most notably the Center for Advanced Study in the Behavioral Sciences at Stanford University, but even they do not follow Flexner's idea exactly.

Flexner had realized that all American universities could not model themselves after his Institute, but he had wanted it to point toward the goal which American higher education should reach. Remote from the cares of practical affairs, scholars were to investigate the unknown and create knowledge capable of vitalizing the world. Their students, trained in the intellectual professions, were to be prepared to implement the latest findings of scholarship into social practice.

In advising against the active involvement of professors in socio-political affairs, however, Flexner took a stronger stand than his model, the German university, would warrant. Throughout the nineteenth and twentieth centuries, German professors had assumed active roles in political matters, but Flexner chose to ignore this. Surprisingly enough, even during the 1930's when many intellectuals were decrying the failure of German professors to resist the inroads of National Socialism, he still called upon academic men to subordinate their civil responsibilities to those of their profession.[42]

In summary, Flexner's insistence that American colleges and universities devote themselves primarily to intellectual pursuits led him to criticize higher education for operational utility. The concept of operational utility had entailed the functioning of society without necessarily devoting attention to the conceptual knowledge upon which actions were predicated. In the instance of general education, much of it indeed failed to assist the student to reach the point of carrying on independent thinking. Regarding vocational education, the preparation of students for jobs likewise did not often develop their ability to carry on original research. Since Flexner wanted both general and vocational education to serve the purposes of research, he properly criticized them.

Contemporary functions of American colleges and universities were aimed at helping society solve its operational needs. Flexner, too, wanted a connection between the studies of the university and the needs of society but not the same kind that advocates of operational utility proposed. Neither they nor Flexner wanted the university to avoid the study of delicate and controversial issues in the social and economic spheres; but rather than university service to society, Flexner wanted the university to serve the advancement of knowledge. If a close connection was to exist between society and the university, the former was simply to serve as a research area for scholars. As already pointed out, he maintained that new academic discoveries would eventually sift back to society and provide the basis for the progress of the whole civilization. Essentially, then, Flexner was arguing that the concept of operational utility might bring short-range advantages. His program of higher education, however, in the long run would bring greater

---

[42]For a valuable study of the fate of higher learning in Germany, see Friedrich Lilge, *The Abuse of Learning: the Failure of the German University* (New York, 1948).

advantages, even in operating techniques. By discovering new facts and principles, not by giving specific directions to men of affairs, the American university could become the most important institution in raising the tone of American life.

Therefore, Flexner shared with Babbitt and Nock a common dislike for the prevailing tendencies of American higher education, but he based his arguments upon a different rationale and proposed different remedies for his diagnosed ills of colleges and universities. He did not desire a return to the nineteenth-century literary college. He wanted to move far from its assumptions and practices. His college would have a curriculum unrelated to the development of character. His collegiate curriculum was to prepare students to enter graduate programs.

Flexner's ideas about the relationship of a university to society in some regards approached those of Babbitt and Nock. Like them he did not want colleges or universities to concern themselves with society's operational problems. He differed from Babbitt and Nock, however, by admitting the worth of the study of economic and political problems if it could add to the development of knowledge. Babbitt and Nock were more concerned with fundamental value commitments than economic and political issues. They would have considered such matters societal veneer. Man's inner, subjective needs, not his outer nonsubjective activities, they argued, were crucial. Babbitt, to be sure, also urged scholarly attention to cultural standards appropriate to the twentieth century. His goal, however, remained the development of character within individuals. Flexner did not express any written concern about the character of the men who would use the new knowledge. Absent from his thought is the overwhelming concern with individual character which characterized the thinking of Babbitt and Nock.

Flexner furthermore clearly did not share Babbitt's and Nock's profoundly conservative views of social change. In fact, Flexner believed that American colleges and universities were too afraid to criticize the ethics, politics, and institutions of the nation. He feared that their commitment to the social, economic, and religious status quo would prevent them from becoming the home of the relentless questioning and criticizing which alone leads to the new facts and concepts basic to expanding knowledge. Perhaps the central theme to all his educational writing is the call for a separation of colleges and universities from the operational problems of their environment, for only a complete freedom from such distractions would enable scholars to deal exclusively with those new facts and concepts. With this advance in nonoperational knowledge, society could progress. Without it, eventual stabilization and decay awaited mankind.

CHAPTER SIX

ROBERT MAYNARD HUTCHINS:
Man's Highest Powers

Nothing is more striking than the absence of connection between the basic problems of America and the educational program of America. Our real needs are to discover how to make democracy work, how to survive in the nuclear age, and what to do with ourselves if we do survive. A system of accommodation cannot help us meet these needs. If we are to meet them, we shall have to dedicate our colleges and universities to the production of disciplined intelligence, and to that alone.

ROBERT MAYNARD HUTCHINS, 1960

ONE OF THE COUNTRY'S most renowned critics of colleges and universities, Robert Maynard Hutchins, stated in the conclusion of his most famous work:

The university . . . is intellectual. It is wholly and completely so. As such, it is the only kind of university worth having. I believe that it will accomplish greater political and professional results than one that is devoted to current events or vocational training.[1]

Earlier in the same book he emphasized that the concept of utility was not in harmony with the intellectual university.

[1] Robert M. Hutchins, *The Higher Learning in America* (New Haven, 1936), p. 118.

133

> *The trouble with the popular notion of utility is that it con-
> fuses immediate and final ends. Material prosperity and
> adjustment to the environment are good more or less, but
> they are not good in themselves and there are other goods
> beyond them. The intellectual virtues, however, are good in
> themselves and good as means to happiness.*[2]

Hutchins may have concurred with the opposition of Babbitt,
Nock, and Flexner to the main trends of contemporary higher
education, but he did not propose an educational program
paralleling any of their disparate ones.   Instead he advocated
a metaphysically ordered higher education based upon his own
faith in rational man and democratic society.

While Flexner had remained silent on social issues and
Babbitt and Nock had favored elitism, Hutchins approved of
an equalitarian, democratic society.   Babbitt and Nock had
believed that most individuals lack the capability to rule themselves, but Hutchins affirmed the reverse.   Moreover, Hutchins
rejected Spencerian notions of the state, for he believed that
modern man can develop only within the framework of a
comprehensive democratic state.   Both Babbitt and Nock
clearly recognized that the individual needs a social group to
realize his potential, but they preferred voluntary organizations,
not the state.

Hutchins' interests reflect in large part his own experience.
His life has been involved primarily with colleges and universities and their relationship to society.   Born in a prosperous
section of Brooklyn, New York, in 1899, he grew up surrounded
by good books, stimulating conversation, and the problems of
educational administration.   His father, a Congregational minister, left the pastoral ministry in Brooklyn and taught at Oberlin
College.   Young Hutchins began his undergraduate career at
Oberlin but interrupted it to serve as an ambulance driver in

---

[2]Hutchins, *ibid.*, p. 62.

World War I. After returning from the war, he entered Yale College and completed his formal education at the Yale Law School. In large part because of his brilliance as a public speaker, while still a law student he became secretary of the corporation of Yale University. After he completed law school in 1925, the Yale Law School unexpectedly needed an instructor and offered him the post. Two years later he became its acting dean and in 1928 its dean.

At this time he had not come to any firm decisions about either educational philosophy or general political and social theory. As dean of the Yale Law School he had, however, doubted the worth of the case method of instruction and desired a substitute. While teaching a course in evidence, he had become disturbed because he could not find valid principles behind judicial decisions. C. K. Ogden, a philosophically oriented psychologist and dean of the graduate school at Cornell, suggested that he talk with a young philosophy instructor at Columbia, Mortimer Adler. At the time Adler was studying legal philosophy, and he made an impact upon Hutchins which shaped the whole direction of Hutchins' subsequent thought.[3]

In 1929 Hutchins, at the age of thirty, became president of the University of Chicago. Soon after assuming the presidency, Hutchins found Adler a position on the faculty of the University's law school. During the first five years at Chicago, Hutchins formulated a theory of higher education which reflected Adler's neo-Aristotelianism, and he has maintained it virtually unchanged to the present day. Like Babbitt and Nock, he thought that the modern world had left its Graeco-Christian tradition and needed new cultural standards. He believed that men could agree upon a metaphysical ordering of knowledge and build a new society upon it.

---

[3]Robert M. Hutchins, *Freedom, Education, and the Fund* (New York, 1956), p. 19, and an interview with Hutchins.

Holding these views, he initiated wide-ranging changes at Chicago which affected the whole university. He thoroughly reorganized the faculty, the course of study, and traditional college life. His abolition of intercollegiate football drew national comment. In making his changes, he thought that the rational ordering of colleges and universities could assist in the reconstruction of all society according to rational metaphysical principles.

In 1951, after more than twenty years of controversy, he left Chicago and became associate director of the Ford Foundation. His ideas about higher education had not only failed to take root on a national scale but had faltered even at Chicago. His experiences had convinced him that colleges and universities could not maintain his standards in the face of a disinterested or hostile social environment. Hence he turned to more direct means of solving the basic problems of American society. Using a fifteen-million-dollar grant from the Ford Foundation, he assisted in founding the Fund for the Republic, which is attempting to analyze the nature of a democratic society. Since assuming the leadership of the Fund in 1954, he has spent the greater part of his time as director of the Fund's major undertaking, The Center for the Study of Democratic Institutions.

RATIONAL MAN AND THE DEMOCRATIC STATE

In order to understand Hutchins' educational and social positions, one must understand his convictions about the nature of man, for like Babbitt and Nock, he built the rest of his thought about his views of man. They form the foundation for the positions he took on most other subjects. From the time his educational ideas took their present shape, a clear philosophy of human nature has run throughout his writings.

Rational Man

The purposes of education do not originate in the educational system. Still less are they determined by the prejudices of educators or of writers on education. They are fixed by the nature of man.[4]

Hutchins accepted the common definition of man as a rational animal. Unlike Nock, who believed that most men were merely beasts, and Babbitt, who felt that the majority of men could not respond to their reason, Hutchins asserted that the intellects of all men give them the capacity for moral, spiritual, and political growth. He further asserted that in spite of differing physical and social environments, the power of intellect remains the same in men throughout the world and enables them to cope with moral and political questions regardless of the surrounding culture.[5] Although very much aware that all men are animals, Hutchins pointed out that all men possess reason, which the other animals lack, and this higher power, as he called reason, in fact defines their humanity.

By stressing the importance of intellect, Hutchins did not mean to exclude other facets of man's personality such as his moral and spiritual potential. He thought that happiness, the end of the good life, depends upon these qualities as much as upon rational powers. Since, however, he posited that the individual cannot acquire or attain these other characteristics without the use of reason, the power of intellect is all-important in his system. Hutchins' position paralleled Babbitt's belief that actions do not result directly from thought, but rather from habit. He asserted, however, that the growth of habits which lead to the development of one's highest powers depends upon

---

[4]Robert M. Hutchins, "T. S. Eliot on Education," *Measure,* I (1950), 8.

[5]Robert M. Hutchins, "Learning to Live," *Ladies Home Journal,* LXIII (1946), 25; Robert M. Hutchins, "Toward a Durable Society" *Fortune,* XXVII (1943), 201.

choices which the individual makes over an extended period. Since choice in turn implies the determination of ends and the means to attain those ends, thinking becomes crucial in the formation of habit. Therefore, in Hutchins' plan the power of intellect is decisive for attaining the good life.

Writing during a century well aware of Freud, Hutchins realized that men are swayed by emotions and desires that must be held in check. He thought, however, that an intellectual grasp of the aims of life and the means of attaining them would guarantee that in times of flux a man would be able to channel his life purposefully, lifting himself above the demands of circumstance. Like Babbitt, Hutchins stressed that thinking can sustain habit when the tumult of life beats upon it. He insisted that constant thought about an individual's experience is necessary if experience is to lead to the development of his moral, spiritual, and intellectual potential.

In light of the importance of reason in Hutchins' view of human nature, the importance of education to him is evident. Education, especially higher education, exists to develop man's ability to think. Thus men need an educational pattern which can help them develop their rational powers. Without the ability to reason properly, they are little more than animals.

The Necessity of the State

In considering man's quest to strengthen his highest powers, Hutchins decided that man is "naturally insufficient and insecure in isolation."[6] He assumed that the individual can only develop within a social group. Opportunities for choice must exist before a person can exercise his choice, and social organization offers these choices. In short, society provides the structure for each citizen to realize his highest powers.

Hutchins' position differs sharply from those of Babbitt and Nock in designating not any society but, more specifically,

---

[6]Robert M. Hutchins, "Legal Education," *Vital Speeches*, March 1, 1937, p. 309.

a political society as the most advantageous form of social organization. He thought that in the modern world only the state could marshal the force needed to ensure the opportunity of all to develop their highest powers. He could not conceive of anyone strengthening his highest powers without the prosperity, peace, and justice which only that final arbiter of force, the state, can provide. Since he believed that all men are still animals, regardless of their level of rationality, he did not, as Babbitt and Nock did, wish to trust anyone with unrestricted power. The state, instead of the Remnant, was to provide for social order.

Hutchins did not share the fear of Babbitt and Nock that the strong state would necessarily destroy the individual. He condemned their Spencerian belief that the government which governs least governs best. Instead he stated: "That government is best which governs best."[7] Writing in 1943, he pronounced that the state need become neither an end in itself, as the Nazis were advocating, nor a referee, as the Liberty Leaguers had been saying.[8] In his opinion the truly democratic state exists to assist its citizens in developing their moral, spiritual, and intellectual powers. A democracy gives everyone the opportunity to participate in the political process, and this activity is necessary for the growth of one's highest powers.

He cautioned that any state could forget its proper function. He believed, for instance, that a state sincerely dedicated to the development of its citizens would provide them opportunities for learning. In fact, he maintained that the good state would hold as its highest function the promotion of the "development of scholarship, the improvement of the professions, and the cultivation of the mind."[9] A state which turned from these to

---

[7]Robert M. Hutchins, "Is Democracy Possible?" *Saturday Review*, Feb. 21, 1959, p. 58.

[8]Robert M. Hutchins. *Education for Freedom* (Baton Rouge, 1943), p. 83.

[9]Hutchins, *Higher Learning in America*, p. 18.

the promotion of other aims could hinder rather than aid the welfare of its citizens.

Pragmatism

As Hutchins observed the American scene, he asserted that the desire for food, shelter, and health had deflected the country from a concentration upon those activities which would strengthen man's highest powers. Instead of human values, Hutchins thought that America honored money. Cherishing money, he stated, her people as a whole were working for the acquisition of material goods by any possible means. Hutchins could not see how a just economic and political society could endure with a rational and emotional commitment to money instead of man's highest powers.

Like Babbitt and Nock, he feared that the nation had substituted industrial power, military strength, and gadgets for the moral, spiritual, and intellectual basis upon which society should rest. Man needs a minimal material level for life, but Hutchins emphasized that man can live a human rather than animal existence only as his higher powers find fulfillment. In his opinion the organization of life about economic considerations destroys human nature, and he called for the subordination of economic purposes to those which enhance man's highest powers. He did not want economic activity to become the end of life but to remain a means of sustaining the moral, spiritual, and intellectual life. The state itself, he cautioned, had to assure the subordination of the economic good of the community to the individual's highest purposes.

Unfortunately, he concluded, America had lost its commitment to humane purposes because pressure groups had come to dominate it. It cared for the welfare of those, he quipped, "well enough organized to put on the pressure."[10] Instead of protecting the citizen from pressure groups, the political community had disintegrated into a struggle between them.

---

[10] Hutchins, "Is Democracy Possible?" p. 58.

Like Babbitt and Nock, he thought that a consensus about political and social ideals was disappearing. He further believed that a lack of commitment to abstract principles was in large part responsible. He blamed men like William James, John Dewey, and Oliver Wendell Holmes, who had been expounding the doctrines of pragmatic realism. He stated that they were teaching the existence of only folkways, not morals. Such a viewpoint leads, he charged, to the pervasive belief that only expediency counts.

With the spread of pragmatic beliefs, Hutchins asserted, force will become the only way of settling differences of opinion. In his own field of law, for example, he denounced the predominant maxims of realistic jurisprudence which held that the law is what the courts say it is. Writing during the 1930's, Hutchins claimed that he could see little difference between such a position and Hitler's dictum that the law is what he does.

In fact, he countered, everything canot be merely a matter of opinion because one man's opinion is not as good as another's. Disciplined thinking, in his judgment, brings conviction based on more than mere prejudice and force of local circumstance. In modern America, he asserted, people lack this disciplined thought, and colleges and universities are not assisting them to develop it. Instead, the pragmatic spirit rules without any intelligible standard of good or bad. Hutchins deplored the legacy of James and similar thinkers because it leads men to concentrate upon operational techniques and gives no answers to questions of ends. Hutchins felt that America in general and higher education in particular had become concerned with means without regard for ends.

In the quest for freedom, for example, Americans had made freedom an end in itself. Instead, he maintained, freedom consists in allowing men the opportunity to develop good moral, spiritual, and intellectual habits. Hutchins called not merely for more freedom to live, but rather for the freedom which men need to develop their highest powers. "Men must be free to exercise those powers which make them men."[11]

Intellectual Power and Democratic Social Change

Hutchins placed his hopes for the creation of his ideal society upon the development in all citizens of the intellectual power capable of discovering metaphysical principles. He believed that if a democratic constituency could possess such power, it could direct itself toward correct goals. Basically, Hutchins reflected the Aristotelianism of Adler when he stated that men could develop themselves only as they apprehended these abstract principles, which he defined as the manifestation of the divine urge within men to perfect themselves.[12] By applying abstract reason to the best thought of mankind, men could perceive the metaphysical laws governing the universe and then use them to approach perfection.

Hutchins distinguished between two kinds of law: natural and conventional. Natural law, he asserted, is common to all the world because human nature is the same everywhere. Conventional law, on the other hand, varies because peculiar circumstances in time and place exist. Conventional law makes justice relative to the circumstances of a society at a given time and place.[13]

The task of improving society, as he saw it, lay in changing the conventional law of a society to approach natural law. By structuring a society in accord with "the perfection possible to men as men," people could construct a society which would open to everyone the choices needed to develop their highest powers.[14]

---

[11]Robert M. Hutchins, "Victory Must Begin at Home!" *Christian Century*, April 29, 1942, p. 555.

[12]Robert M. Hutchins, *St. Thomas and the World State* (Milwaukee, 1949) , p. 38.

[13]Hutchins, "Legal Education," pp. 309-310.

[14]Hutchins, *St. Thomas*, p. 38.

Hutchins explained mankind's failure to adhere to natural law by recalling that man possesses animal as well as rational characteristics. Hence Hutchins emphasized the importance of properly organized colleges and universities. They were to train the intellectual powers so that man might live by his rational rather than animal side. Without intellectual power a man cannot be wise, for wisdom is the habit of using reason to grasp the first principles which form the basis of universal judgments.[15]

If men cannot use abstract reason to grasp the principles of natural law, asserted Hutchins, they would only be able to establish conventional laws observable to their senses. They would only be able to discover the laws peculiar to their own time and place. Thus society could not reflect the order of the universe. How could men institute natural law if they did not perceive its principles?

Admitting that no experimental verification of natural law is possible, Hutchins placed his faith in man's ability to reach these laws solely through the exercise of his intellectual powers. He maintained that only the so-called disciplined mind could perceive natural law and hence cope with the problems of society.

His views assumed democratic overtones because of his belief that everyone except morons could acquire intellectual power. Hutchins' commitment to democracy contrasts sharply to the ideas of Babbitt and Nock. His ideas reflect none of their aristocratic social theories. Elites of any form, in his opinion, represent a threat to democracy, and he opposed them. He condemned as "aristocracy with a vengeance" the notion that the majority of mankind cannot attain the degree of mental discipline necessary for self rule.[16] The very idea of a Remnant was foreign to this thinking, for he continually asserted that all

---

[15]Robert M. Hutchins, "The University and Character," *Commonweal,* April 22, 1938, p. 710.

[16]Robert M. Hutchins, *The Great Conversation* (Chicago, 1952), p. 48.

men can develop their intellectual powers to the point needed to exercise intelligent citizenship. He in fact defined the ideal democratic community by the extent to which each citizen possesses intellectual power and exercises it in important political decisions affecting his life.[17]

Hutchins actually took a more egalitarian position than the Wisconsin professors, who wanted the university to provide experts for technical bodies, for he distrusted even groups of specialists such as the Wisconsin commissions.

> *To the extent to which all governmental operations are esoteric and all important matters with which government deals are available only to technicians or specialists or comprehensible by them, to that extent the citizen, unless there is an admirable educational system and perfect media of mass communication, is unlikely to be able to engage in intelligent discussion of the most important political issues.*[18]

Strangely enough, Hutchins perceived the same problem as the proponents of the Wisconsin Idea. They too had realized that experts might pose a danger to democracy. Their variety of general education, for example, was to equip everyone in the state to understand the immediate problems of government and hence be able to control the policy decisions behind governmental operation. Hutchins, on the other hand, was concerned with broad philosophical matters, and he never dealt with the question of how citizens could understand operational matters if they did not study them. His notion of intelligent understanding of government differed sharply from those of the proponents of operational utility.

While the men at the University of Wisconsin had been concerned with transmitting operational information about

---

[17]Robert M. Hutchins, *The Political Animal* (Santa Barbara, 1962), p. 2.

[18]Hutchins, *ibid.*, p. 5.

contemporary affairs to their students, the government, and the general population, Hutchins wanted the university to develop in its students the ability to understand "the order of goods and achieve them in their order."[19] With this intellectual power, in Hutchins' view, the individual could then "operate well in all fields and deal with new problems as they arise."[20] Citizens could then grasp the principles of natural law and understand the criteria upon which political decisions should rest. By developing the rational powers of men, colleges and universities could produce the intelligence upon which a rational, democratic society had to rest. The sole task of higher education, as he saw it, lay in making "rational animals more perfectly rational."[21] The application of that intelligence to the operational problems of the contemporary scene was none of their concern.

COLLEGES AND UNIVERSITIES FOR INTELLECTUAL POWER

As Hutchins observed the dreadful obligations facing America during the Great Depression, the crises of World War II, and the frustrations of the Cold War, he concluded that most colleges and universities were simply not teaching people to think on the level necessary for mankind's survival. He charged that colleges and universities were not developing the intellectual powers of their students. Instead of devotion to the intellect, he saw factual research absorbing the interest of the faculty and social life that of the students. With such a situation he complained that colleges and universities obstruct

---

[19]Robert M. Hutchins, "Reintegration of the University," *University of Chicago Magazine,* XXIX (1937) , 89.

[20]Robert M. Hutchins, "Education for Democracy," *School and Society,* June 18, 1949, p. 428.

[21]Hutchins, *Education for Freedom,* p. 37.

rather than aid a democracy to order itself in accordance with metaphysical principles.

As he studied the condition of both private and public colleges and universities, he asked whether they had not abandoned all serious claims to intellectual leadership in the United States. He feared that instead of providing a light for a dark world, they mirrored its chaos. Triviality and mediocrity marred every college and university campus he knew. They were, he felt, characterized by skepticism, presentism, scientism, and antiintellectualism. He could not see how institutions with such values could fashion the intellect. He believed that an abiding faith in the intellect is necessary before colleges and universities can develop the intellectual power of their students.

As an administrator of a major university, he asserted that intellectual problems were causing most of the inadequacies of higher education. Even during the depression, he claimed that the rational ordering of the University of Chicago, not financial worries, constituted his most serious concern.

Separation of the College from the University

Like Flexner, Hutchins felt that American institutions of higher learning could promote the development of intellect better if the college and university were separated from one another. Both thought that the adoption of graduate work by many colleges in the late nineteenth century had created confusion. In their opinions the traditional orientation of the American college toward general education and the focus of the newer graduate schools upon specialized education and research did not blend well.

Hutchins did not propose, as had Flexner, that colleges direct their curricula toward graduate education. Vocational objectives played no part in his collegiate plans. He wanted the contemporary college to concentrate on one thing only: the development of the intellectual power of the student. This could be done, he insisted, by introducing the student to the basic ideas of his civilization and by giving him the techniques necessary to understand them. He believed that the study of the wisdom of the human race would bring the student to an awareness of his own place in that tradition.

In a vein similar to Babbitt and Nock, Hutchins urged a concentration upon great literature, for he believed that the individual could not grasp standards of social criticism and action without it. He took sharp issue with thinkers who recommended the direct study of social problems as a means for preparing the students to deal with them. Hutchins said that the best education even for public life "is a thorough knowledge of the moral and political wisdom accumulated through our intellectual history."[22]

> *I shall not be attentive when you tell me that the plan of general education I am about to present is remote from real life, that real life is in constant flux and change, and that education must be in constant flux and change as well. I do not deny that all things are in change. . . . But we are so impressed with scientific and technological progress that we assume similar progress in every field. . . . Our erroneous notion of progress has thrown the classics and the liberal arts out of the curriculum, overemphasized the empirical sciences, and made education the servant of any contemporary movements in society, no matter how superficial.*[23]

He held that students who understand the great books will both desire and be able to contribute to society's improvement. Possessing not the tricks of the trade, but intellectual power, they will be able to solve new problems as they arise and "remold the environment to make it conform to the aspirations of the human spirit."[24]

---

[22]Robert M. Hutchins, "The Colleges and Public Service," *Bulletin of the Association of American Colleges,* XXIV (1938), 35.

[23]Hutchins, *Higher Learning in America,* pp. 64-65.

[24]Hutchins, *Freedom, Education, and the Fund,* p. 143.

When he stated that the college should give the student the necessary techniques to understand the great ideas, he meant specifically the techniques of thinking, reading, and writing. Since logic deals with thinking, and rhetoric and grammar with reading and writing, Hutchins wanted every student to master logic, rhetoric, and grammar. He also included mathematics in the curriculum because he believed it also teaches people to think. If other subjects also develop the students' ability to think, read, and write, Hutchins said he would not object to their inclusion in the course of study.

He did not take the same view as Nock of the disciplinary value of the classics as taught in nineteenth-century America. In his opinion, the teachers of the classics had destroyed the interest of their students in great books because they concentrated upon points of grammar rather than upon ideas.[25] Neither did Hutchins advocate that American higher education adopt the trivium and quadrivium as understood in the Middle Ages.[26] He wanted the student to become aware of the approach of great thinkers to significant problems by reading the most important books written in Western civilization.[27]

The great books, along with logic, grammar, rhetoric, and mathematics, constituted the main part of Hutchins' curriculum. He did not criticize the teaching of religious, artistic, musical, and physical education, but he insisted that they not deflect the college from its central task: the development of intellectual power.

---

[25]Hutchins, *Great Conversation*, p. 27.

[26]Robert M. Hutchins, "Tradition in Education," *Vital Speeches*, Feb. 15, 1938, p. 258.

[27]At Chicago, Hutchins and his associates, notably Mortimer Adler, drew up a list of these books. They appeared in 1952 under the title "Great Books of the Western World." The Encyclopaedia Britannica Company, affiliated with the University of Chicago, marketed them throughout the country. See George Ernest Arnstein, "The Great Books Program and its Educational Philosophy" (Doctoral dissertation, University of California, 1953).

He also made clear that whatever was included in the curriculum should be required for every student. Along with Babbitt, Nock, and to a degree Flexner, he maintained that unrestricted elective systems deny that any specific content exists for higher education. He blamed elective systems for the lack of understanding which educated men have among themselves.[28]

Hutchins wanted every American to study his recommended subjects and hence advocated the enrollment in the college of everyone between the ages of sixteen and twenty. He consistently maintained that with the proper familial and social environments, every person could develop the mental ability to attend college. To elitists who believed that only a select few could benefit from collegiate education, Hutchins retorted that only the proof of students failing in the classroom would convince him of his error.

He did agree with the elitists that only the better students should continue from the college to the university. In a plan similar to Flexner's, Hutchins wanted the university to become a place where all professors and all students would be engaged in individual study devoted to the advancement of conceptual thought. Only the brilliant could participate in this adventure.

In contrast to the college, Hutchins' university would exist solely to find and communicate the metaphysical principles which would enable man to understand his social and natural environment. By this conceptual research, Hutchins felt, the university could furnish the college with the basic ideas to be communicated to the young. Hutchins assumed that the university like the college would carry on teaching. He wanted the university to educate only people who were grappling in a conceptual manner with the fundamental principles of the social and natural world.[29]

---

[28]Hutchins, *Freedom, Education, and the Fund*, p. 133.

[29]Robert M. Hutchins, "The Issue in the Higher Learning," *International Journal of Ethics*, XLIV (1934), 182.

Hutchins did not consider science, even in its best conceptual form, equal to philosophy. Although he never renounced his belief that science represents the greatest accomplishment of modern times, he did not think that it is directly relevant to the questions most important to him: those of value. He maintained that scientific empiricism cannot lead men to basic goals. It gives means, not ends.[30]

Hutchins called instead for a new integrative scholarship which would bring "to bear upon the life of its time the accumulated wisdom of the race, including science . . . and . . . promote a wiser and deeper understanding of man, his world, and his destiny."[31]   This, the central obligation of a university as Hutchins perceived it, would bring man closer to an understanding of the natural laws governing the universe and give him the intellectual tools to construct his own society in accord with them.

Universities, Not Service Stations

Clearly Hutchins rejected the idea of organizing American higher education to satisfy society's wish for education of operational utility.   Only a focus upon metaphysical principles could give "unity, intelligibility, and meaning" to the university's work.[32]   He emphasized that university scholars should study topics of contemporary relevance only to illuminate these abstract principles.   Efforts to solve operational problems belonged in research institutes not integrally related to a university.   Such research centers had to remain apart from the university proper.   Too close a relationship would only distract the university from its proper purpose.   University

---

[30]Robert M. Hutchins, *No Friendly Voice* (Chicago, 1936), p. 34.

[31]Robert M. Hutchins, "Unanswered Questions," *University of Chicago Magazine*, XXXVII (1945), 5.

[32]Robert M. Hutchins, "The Next Fifty Years," *Science*, XCIV (1941), 335.

professors and students should not be bothered with matters irrelevant to metaphysical principles.

An institution catering to the immediate needs of its social environment, he remarked, is no university, but rather a "service station for the community."[33] The notion of making colleges and universities institutions of operational utility through extension services, for example, repelled him.

According to this conception a university must make itself felt in the community; it must be constantly, currently felt. A state university must help the farmers look after their cows. An endowed university must help adults get better jobs by giving them courses in the afternoon and evening. Yet it is apparent that the kind of professors that are interested in these objects may not be the kind that are interested either in developing education or in advancing knowledge. Since a university will not be able to have two kinds of professors and at the same time remain clear as to what it is about, it must follow that extension work can only confuse the institution.[34]

Like Nock and Flexner and in contrast to Babbitt, Hutchins did not object to the study of matters of operational utility. He simply objected to their intrusion into American colleges and universities. These men were essentially monists. Each proposed one purpose for colleges and universities, and none of them wanted higher education for operational utility to deflect attention from what each considered the one proper purpose of higher learning in America.

Like Babbitt, Nock, and Flexner, he wrote disparagingly against courses within the university which attempted to fit students for jobs in the nonacademic world. The training of

---

[33]Hutchins, *Freedom, Education, and the Fund,* p. 117.

[34]Hutchins, *Higher Learning in America,* pp. 6-7.

automobile drivers and beauty operators had no place in his curriculum. He thought that vocationalism disrupts the ordering of higher education according to rational principles. He recognized that people have to be trained for jobs, but he thought that vocational training simply confuses efforts to make universities effective institutions for developing the intellect. It does not, therefore, belong in the university.

Vocationalism leads, then, to triviality and isolation; it debases the course of study and the staff. It deprives the university of its only excuse for existence, which is to provide a haven where the search for truth may go on unhampered by utility or pressure for "results."[35]

In Hutchins' opinion, vocational education teaches a student how to exist but not how to live. Reflecting a Platonic bias, he called it the education of bondsmen and slaves. He condemned it as undemocratic because everyone in a democracy deserves the education of a freeman. An educational system dedicated to increasing vocational technique could not, in Hutchins' terms, produce the wisdom needed to guide modern society.[36]

Taking the same position as Flexner, Hutchins caustically stated that money plays an important role in higher education for operational utility.

Undoubtedly the love of money and that sensitivity to public demands that it creates has a good deal to do with the service-station conception of a university.[37]

Nevertheless, Hutchins urged professors to contribute to society any results of their research with practical significance. He warned that the universities of Germany during the 1930's

---

[35]Hutchins, *ibid.*, p. 43.

[36]Robert M. Hutchins, *The University of Utopia* (Chicago, 1953), p. 13.

[37]Hutchins, *Higher Learning in America*, p. 6.

stand as examples of what happens when the university isolates itself from the basic conceptual study upon which the world of affairs ultimately depends. Society would force the university to abstain from thinking which borders in any way upon vital issues of the day. Hutchins never wrote in favor of scholars studying operational problems of society, but he did urge a close tie between the conceptual thinking characteristic of a university and the problems of society. He thought that the synthetic, generalized thinking about fundamental issues possible in the university could aid society.[38]

During the Second World War he violated this idea when he authorized the use of University of Chicago scientists on the Manhattan Project. The atomic bomb was developed in a laboratory under the University's football stadium. This undertaking obviously went into areas of operational utility. Yet he declared that the university itself should never become directly involved in practical affairs. In his judgment, such a situation would lead merely to the subjection of the university to outside interests. He did not think that the service ideal would bring service to the state anyway.

The service-station conception means not so much that the University serves the state as that it serves any group in the state that has the votes.[39]

Since he thought that pressure groups hindered the United States from becoming a true democracy, he did not identify contemporary majority rule with the real interests of all the people. Since the state consists of all the people, the wishes of pressure groups were not necessarily an expression of the best interests of the state.

---

[38]Robert M. Hutchins, "The University and the Mind of the Ages," *Measure,* I (1950) , 140. Hutchins, "Unanswered Questions," pp. 3 ff.

[39]Robert M. Hutchins, *The State of the University,* 1929-1949 (Chicago, 1949) , p. 12.

The university would accomplish far more for the advancement of all society, he maintained, if it would remain solely a community of scholars, not a political party or a propaganda agency. The intellectual university, the only one he considered worth having, would yield greater social benefits than the one devoted to the study of current events. Centers of independent thought would give the world a better chance of surviving, he believed.

Hutchins especially lamented the use of general education for purposes of operational utility. Intellectual power was far more relevant to what he considered the real needs of society than the knowledge conveyed in most collegiate curricula. Like Babbitt, Nock, and Flexner, he argued that his plans would eventually result in the greatest utility for the student.

> *The scheme that I advance is based on the notion that general education . . . will not be useful to [the student] outside the university in the popular sense of utility. It may not assist him to make money or to get ahead. It may not in any obvious fashion adjust him to his environment or fit him for the contemporary scene. It will, however, have a deeper, wider utility: it will cultivate the intellectual virtues.[40]*

Hutchins' enmity toward the concept of operational utility arose because of his deep feelings about the importance of intellectual virtues. Without the ability to reason abstractly, men could never perceive metaphysical principles. The society of greatest benefit to man had to rest upon these principles. If myopic views about higher education hindered the search for them, society would eventually suffer. For these reasons, Hutchins struggled to implement an educational program aimed at developing the intellectual powers.

---

[40]Hutchins, *Higher Learning in America*, p. 62.

Attempts at Implementation

During his years at the University of Chicago, Hutchins attempted to build an educational institution to conform with his ideas.[41] Soon after arriving in Chicago, he approved a plan already developed there which required a standard curriculum of integrated courses for all students enrolled in the college. Furthermore, the college was reorganized to include students from the traditional junior year of high school through the sophomore year of college. The student received a certificate at the end of the sophomore year and was then free to enter the university proper.

As Hutchins developed his own educational theories, he was coming to favor a curriculum consisting of about one hundred great books and little else. The faculty of the University of Chicago balked at the great-books plan, and Hutchins was never able to see it adopted there. At St. John's College in Annapolis, Maryland, however, where Hutchins was a member of the board, he and some of his Chicago supporters got a more nearly "pure" version of the great-books plan established by the end of World War II. At Chicago, Hutchins did not try to include the extensive work in classical languages required at St. John's, but along with the designers of the St. John's plan, he believed that the great books would quicken the intellectual power of students.

In spite of his lack of success regarding the great books at Chicago, he did gain approval of another revolutionary proposal. In 1942 he succeeded in splitting the traditional four-year undergraduate program completely in half. In a close contest in which Hutchins cast the deciding vote, the faculty

---

[41]The following information dealing with the University of Chicago came from several persons high in its administration, including the Board of Trustees. For a good account of the development of the Chicago program, see Reuben Frodin's "Very Simple, but Thoroughgoing," in the book by seventeen faculty members of the College of the University of Chicago, *The Idea and Practice of General Education* (Chicago, 1950).

dropped the junior and senior years from the college and approved awarding baccalaureate degrees at the end of the sophomore year. Another educational practice which had been initiated at Chicago earlier, namely, the granting of credit for examinations passed rather than courses taken, enabled a student to receive the bachelor's degree in a minimum of time.

As might be imagined, these changes aroused the ire of the traditional four-year colleges throughout the land. If the bachelor's degree were to be given at the end of the sophomore year, such colleges would probably disappear. High schools would most likely enlarge their programs to include the first two years of college, and universities would absorb the last two. Junior colleges already existed in California adjacent to high schools. If allowed to grant the B.A. degree, high schools might easily assume the functions of the college which Hutchins was proposing. A number of four-year college adminstrators and professors called Chicago's new B.A. degree the "bastard degree."

Hutchins thought he could overcome the opposition of the traditional colleges if other major American universities would follow his lead. During the early 1940's he believed that the Chicago plan would become the national pattern. The other universities did not follow him, however, and they left Hutchins and the University of Chicago standing alone.

In the 1930's Hutchins had initiated a number of other striking educational changes. The plan he approved upon becoming president of the University of Chicago checked the traditional independence of the academic departments and grouped them into four divisions: the humanities, the social sciences, the biological sciences, and the physical sciences. Together with the college and the professional schools these constituted the organization known as the University of Chicago. Causing a great controversy, he also severed the connection between the University and one of its two medical schools, the Rush Medical Center. Reflecting his concern for conceptual rather than empirical research, he attempted to appoint theorists rather than factually oriented investigators to new faculty positions. The law school, for example, shifted from the preparation of students for the direct practice of law to a curriculum designed to develop in students an understanding of the philosophy of law.

Hutchins believed that these proposals would place the University of Chicago in the forefront of American higher education. In actuality, they did not. For example, Hutchins thought that his accelerated academic program surrounded by an intellectual atmosphere devoid of collegiate irrelevancies such as football would draw the brightest students of the country to Chicago. This did not happen. True, many gifted intellectuals did come, but the University lost its attraction for many bright and socially inclined students.

Not only students stayed away. All of Hutchins' proposals had aroused bitter controversy among the faculty, and over the course of years many scholars left the University. Among other things, Hutchins had attempted to control outside consulting by requiring that all income from nonuniversity academic efforts be given to the University. This included such monies as those obtained as honorariums for speaking engagements. Many faculty members resented his personal style of leadership and found his educational policies inimical to their views.

Of perhaps more ominous portent, some alumni and wealthy donors also turned from the University. The abolition of football had alienated many alumni. Moreover, Hutchins himself, although usually gracious and charming, occasionally impressed others as being supercilious, caustic, and hostile, and he created misunderstandings among some wealthy friends of the University. The contributions which continued to come to the University usually went to the professional schools. The college received little financial support from the community.

In December 1951 his resignation took the University by surprise. Hutchins had reached the end of his tether. The University needed fresh leadership. Lawrence Kimpton, Hutchins' successor, faced three major problems: pacifying the faculty, balancing the budget, and clearing the city slums from the environs of the University. The spiritual wounds felt by the faculty had become too deep for Hutchins to heal. The desertion of wealthy donors had meant that even the repayment of emergency endowment funds used during the hard times of the Great Depression was difficult. Hutchins could not persuade his own board and those responsible for the policies of the city of Chicago to control the city's slums, which were proving such a blight upon the University.

Hutchins could design a constitution for world government, but Hyde Park lay disintegrating at his doorstep. A firm, dedicated advocate of rights for Black people, Hutchins had to view Black pickets protesting living conditions in University-owned slums. He could not implement effective plans to meet his practical problems. Nor did he have a viable program to transform the rest of his educational doctrines into a living reality. Therefore he lost his faith in the ability of American colleges and universities to cope with the cultural crisis which he proclaimed was threatening Western civilization.

As Hutchins' attempts to reform the University of Chicago and the rest of American higher education began to falter, he warned that if the university cannot perform its intellectual function, another institution free of the tradition of American colleges and universities would have to do it.[42] After leaving Chicago, Hutchins concluded that a new kind of educational organization was indeed necessary. With the support of the Fund for the Republic he founded the Center for the Study of

---

[42]Hutchins, *Freedom, Education, and the Fund*, p. 151.

Democratic Institutions, now located in Santa Barbara, California, in which he intends to sponsor basic thought about the nature of contemporary life. He wants it "to illuminate the whole educational system and the speculative and practical issues that confront speculative thinkers and men of action."[43] There, Hutchins hopes to contribute to the shaping of a democratic society through the basic thinking which he feels universities should be doing. Whether the Center for the Study of Democratic Institutions will work an impact upon the nation and thereby prove the validity of Hutchins' conception of the societal role of the university remains to be seen.[44]

Higher Education for Intellectual Power

Quite clearly, Hutchins shared with Babbitt, Nock, and Flexner an antipathy toward the idea of higher education for operational utility. With them, he thought that colleges and universities should concern themselves with other matters. At the same time, he did not base his arguments upon the same grounds as any of the other three. His beliefs about metaphysical principles placed his thought on a path which diverged from theirs.

Perhaps, of the three other men examined so far in this study, Babbitt's position most fundamentally resembles Hutchins'. Both laid the cause of society's unrest to the devaluation of the traditional Graeco-Christian faith, and they thought that universities should search for new viable standards. In this search lay their primary goal for colleges and universities, and they opposed the dominant concern of American colleges and universities with matters of operational utility.

Hutchins did not assume, however, as did Babbitt and Nock, that a proper program of higher education could result

---

[43]Hutchins, *University of Utopia,* p. 41.

[44]See *The Printed Word: A Ten-Year Bibliography of the Fund for the Republic and the Center for the Study of Democratic Institutions, 1954-1963* (Santa Barbara, 1964).

in the formation of character. In this respect his ideas approach those of Flexner. Both Hutchins and Flexner stated that the university should be completely intellectual. Both thought that colleges and universities would satisfy their responsibility to students with an intellectual training devoid of the trappings of concern for personality or character. Of course, Hutchins' position differed from that of Flexner because Flexner did not maintain that the search for knowledge would result in the discovery of metaphysical principles.

Hutchins, however, did. His assumption of the existence of a metaphysical ordering of knowledge almost took theological overtones, but Hutchins recognized that theology itself could not provide the principles about which to model the University of Chicago. Most faculty members would not agree on the nature, let alone existence, of God, and thus Hutchins devised a secular, rational system to serve as the idea of his university.

To adopt such a position in 1930 as the president of one of America's most distinguished universities took courage. Supposedly the revolution away from formalism in American thought had occurred decades earlier.[45] Restructuring a major twentieth-century university to meet the requirements of formalistic metaphysical principles might well appear anachronistic. If the best American thinkers had indeed disproved the relevancy of formalistic thought to society, Hutchins was committing a grave error in forcing the intellectual resources of the University of Chicago into the quest for its principles. On the other hand, recent American thinkers of distinction once opposed to formalism have turned again to the search for rational laws.[46] The question of the validity of rational metaphysical principles is far from settled. Like Babbitt,

---

[45]See the penetrating discussion in Morton White, *Social Thought in America* (Boston, 1957), especially Chapter Two.

[46]White, *ibid.*, pp. 247 ff.

Hutchins may in some distant day be seen as a leader in the attempt to save American civilization from relativism and disintegration.

Evidence is lacking, however, that the study of great books develops an ability to perceive the metaphysical structuring of the universe, even if it does exist. Until such proof comes forth, the makers of educational policy probably will continue to remain skeptical of Hutchins' views.

His own experience in higher education seems to confirm the current triumph of the advocates of educational operational utility. Hutchins himself has admitted that he sees little possibility of anyone establishing what he considers a rational system of higher education in America. Thus in a sense he shares Nock's gloom for the future of civilization. In 1946 before his fate at Chicago was sealed, he stated,

> *Civilization can only be saved by a moral, intellectual, and spiritual revolution. If American education can contribute to this revolution, then it offers real hope of salvation to suffering humanity everywhere. If it cannot or will not contribute, then it is irrelevant, and its fate is immaterial.*[47]

Growth of the great-books programs at Shimer College, St. Mary's College of California, and the St. John's Colleges reveals a continuing interest in the great books as a collegiate curriculum. Montieth College of Wayne State University also follows much of the spirit of Hutchins. The few hundred students in these colleges, however, appear insignificant compared to the millions enrolled in the kind of colleges and universities which Hutchins disliked. True, many of the outstanding men associated with Hutchins at Chicago have made a significant impact upon American education. For example, much of the improvement of American high schools in the 1950's came about through the efforts of men like Clarence Faust, at

---

[47]Robert M. Hutchins, "Let's Split the Education Atom," *Collier's,* Dec. 7, 1946, p. 80.

the time president of the Fund for the Advancement of Education and formerly dean of the College of the University of Chicago. Nevertheless, American colleges and universities themselves for the most part have not redirected themselves along the path charted by Hutchins.

Just what does the search for principles mean in a democratic society? Common principles must permeate the body politic to facilitate the consensus necessary for democratic action. This Hutchins recognized. But why need the American community find its common beliefs in metaphysical principles? Babbitt's standards, Flexner's new knowledge, or for that matter any commonly accepted beliefs might also create the needed community.

Yet, Hutchins recognized that goals beyond means are needed. Today a general aimlessness indeed seems to permeate Western civilization. A certain dismay plagues contemporary man about his proper purpose. Hutchins was concerned about ends, and for this he deserves commendation. Whether his proposals can supply such ends, however, is another matter. No evidence exists that they can. On the other hand, no full-fledged commitment to them has proved they cannot.

CHAPTER SEVEN

ALEXANDER MEIKLEJOHN:
Democracy and Social Intelligence

I believe in setting learning apart from life and keeping it there, that it may be pure and true and clean and free . . . the greatest danger to the American college today is that it will be drawn into the common life.

ALEXANDER MEIKLEJOHN, 1923

ALEXANDER MEIKLEJOHN believed that the college, standing apart from its social environment, should develop in its students the intelligence to become responsible citizens of a democratic society. He criticized the status quo in higher education because it was incompatible with his vision for higher education. Like the advocates of higher education for operational utility, he believed that students should receive a general education oriented to contemporary society, but he viewed this as philosophical rather than operational. Like Babbitt, Nock, Flexner, and Hutchins, he thought that American society needed institutions of higher learning remote from operational concerns.

His position developed over a lifetime involved in collegiate teaching, administration, and experimentation. Born in 1872 in England, he came to the United States at the age of eight with his parents and was educated in American schools. He began his professional career in 1897 as an instructor in philosophy at his alma mater, Brown University. By 1901 he had become dean of the University. This position entailed somewhat more responsibility than that of a modern dean of students and gave Meiklejohn valuable administrative experience. He succeeded so well that in 1912 Amherst College chose him as its new president. He served Amherst twelve years and transformed it from a relaxed, comfortable institution for young gentlemen into an academic powerhouse. He introduced the first of the now common survey courses in the social sciences and greatly improved the quality of the faculty.

Animosity on the part of the faculty members whom Meiklejohn was attempting to dislodge finally came to a climax in 1923. This, together with misunderstandings about his personal expenses, resulted in his dismissal. Although the younger professors and the majority of the students supported him, the trustees and the majority of the faculty prevailed, and Meiklejohn left Amherst.

He then wrote articles advocating educational reform and experimentation. As a result he stayed in the national limelight. Because of Meiklejohn's reputation as an educational reformer, Glenn Frank, the open-minded president of the University of Wisconsin, invited him to create a two-year experimental college on the Madison campus. Both thought that a college with nonoperational objectives might well flourish in a modern university.

The Experimental College became the object of animosity on the Wisconsin campus, however, and in 1933 it was discontinued. The attempt at coexistence had failed for a number of reasons. The college had attracted many nonconformist students who did not mingle well with regular students at the University. Their shabby dress and supercilious air irritated many among the general faculty and student body. Since the Experimental College did not possess any buildings of its own, much coordination with the University was necessary, and friction developed at almost all points of contact between the two. Even the faculty of Meiklejohn's college did not harmonize well with that of the

University of Wisconsin proper. The regular faculty of the University had disliked the intrusion of Meiklejohn and his faculty onto the campus, and its resentment resulted in a denial of Meiklejohn's request that his original five-year educational experiment be extended. After the dissolution of the college, Meiklejohn stayed on as a professor of philosophy until he retired in 1938.

During his career in higher education, he had become convinced that colleges and universities could not operate outside the limits set by society at large, and so he became interested in education for the general population. After the failure of the Wisconsin Experimental College in 1933, he established a pioneer adult study agency in San Francisco, The School of Social Studies. Until 1938 he divided his time between this school and the philosophy department in Madison.

In San Francisco he organized his curriculum along the same general lines as that of the Experimental College. He had small groups of about fifteen people meet weekly to discuss some of the great books of the Western heritage. In no way practical, the readings were aimed at giving the student an understanding of the principles underlying modern society.

The School continued until the Second World War. It had never possessed substantial financial resources, and with the coming of the war it simply could not meet its budget. Moreover public interest in it dwindled, and the number of enrolled students did not warrant its continuation. The failure of wealthy San Franciscans to contribute to the School disappointed Meiklejohn, but he had no other choice than to close its doors.

He then turned his energies to civil rights. During the war and afterwards, Meiklejohn had become disturbed about intrusions upon political liberty. Through numerous books, articles, pamphlets, and speeches, he attempted to impress the public with the importance of freedom for a democratic society. The loyalty oath controversy at the University of California during the early 1950's found him in the forefront of the defenders of academic freedom. He wrote a number of articles and pamphlets explaining the basic necessity for academic freedom.[1] In 1957 the American Association of University Professors honored him for his work by naming its academic freedom award after him. His distinguished service in the cause of an open society further earned him the newly created Presidential Medal of Freedom which President Kennedy bestowed upon him in 1963.

INTELLIGENCE

During his entire career, Meiklejohn stated that all men should strive for the attainment of one end: intelligence. When he arrived at Amherst in 1912, for instance, he found a controversy waging between the traditionally oriented advocates of education for character and the more progressive proponents of education for intelligence. He took a strong position favoring the latter and encouraged faculty members to intensify their attention to intelligence. In fact, through his reiteration of this theme, he almost made the cultivation of intelligence a moral obligation. Meiklejohn defined intelligence as conscious control of one's human environment. Revealing a basic optimism which pervaded all his work, he affirmed man's ability and responsibility "to take the world as it is and to make of it, so far as possible, what we wish it to be."[2]

---

[1]Alexander Meiklejohn, "Integrity of the Universities—How to Defend it," *Bulletin of the Atomic Scientists,* IX (1953), 193-194; Alexander Meiklejohn, "The Priority of the Market Place of Ideas," in Law School of the University of Chicago, *Conference on Freedom and the Law,* Conference Series, No. 13, May 7, 1953, pp. 3-15; Alexander Meiklejohn, "Sedition Circa 400 B.C.," *Nation,* April 23, 1955, pp. 349-353; Alexander Meiklejohn, "Should Communists Be Allowed to Teach?" *New York Times Magazine,* March 27, 1949, pp. 10, 64-66; Alexander Meiklejohn, "The Teaching of Intellectual Freedom," *Bulletin of the AAUP,* XXXVIII (1952), 10-25.

[2]Alexander Meiklejohn, *Education Between Two Worlds* (New York, 1942), pp. 263-264.

Like Hutchins, he believed that human life reaches its highest levels only as a person becomes conscious master of his own experience. Meiklejohn thought that everyone, by seeing himself in terms of those things which are worth being and doing, could then choose experiences which would lead him to those ends. This basic core of personal experience, Meiklejohn wrote, would create the unity and direction needed for individual stability in a world of chaos and conflict. Colleges should develop in their students this ability to understand themselves.

Meiklejohn's position differed from Hutchins'. Hutchins maintained that man's intellectual power is independent of place and time. Meiklejohn held that social intelligence is not an innate characteristic of all men. Instead it develops through an intellectual interaction between men and their cultural environment. While Hutchins' intellectual power was a manifestation of human nature, Meiklejohn's social intelligence, in contrast, reflected an ability to make choices in a given situation. Hence education should not be the same in all places and at all times. Rather it should prepare a student to understand the underlying philosophical issues of a particular culture.

Reflecting the same basic conservatism as Babbitt and Nock, he believed that culture itself consists of uncounted experiences passed on to successive generations almost by osmosis. Unlike Babbitt and Nock, however, he revealed his liberality with the assertion that the right education can enable anyone to develop an understanding of a culture's blind, unconscious biases. Meiklejohn's college was to develop this. No other functions were to hinder it from fulfilling this mission.

DEMOCRACY AND INTELLIGENCE

Like Babbitt, Nock, and Flexner, Meiklejohn thought that great differences exist in men's intellectual potential. He shared Hutchins' conviction that the American system of government rests upon the assumption that all men possess the capacity for understanding political issues. He could not see how democracy can exist unless all the people are able and willing to puzzle over it, question it, and deal with its apparent dilemmas and contradictions. He wanted everyone to participate in government.

Concurring with the position of men like the Wisconsin progressives, he stated that the complexities of a technological age demand the use of expert advisory and administrative bodies. He saw nothing contradictory between this stand and the assertion that all men have to participate in the political process, for he believed that basic philosophical choices, not technical decisions, are decisive. As long as the electorate can understand ideological issues, they need not comprehend operational matters.

Unfortunately he never dealt with the question of the extent to which technical options determine the nature of policy choices. He simply stated that although experts might recommend, the people dispose. "We, the people, are governed, directly or indirectly, only by ourselves."[3] "We govern the United States."[4]

These democratic political assumptions explain in part Meiklejohn's great concern for the future of education in America. In his opinion the destiny of the country rests in large part upon the ability of the people to understand national ideology. He believed that this philosophical understanding comes from proper study, and therefore he wanted society to require everyone to receive an education. Unless the people possessed a thorough knowledge of the fundamentals involved in politics, Meiklejohn feared that uninformed opinion would rule in America. Information without the foundation of a

---

[3]Meiklejohn, "Teaching of Intellectual Freedom," p. 16.

[4]Meiklejohn, *ibid.*, p. 21.

rigorous sociopolitical philosophy, he warned, would not become the intelligence needed by the majority in a democratic society. He did not believe that education in the United States had yet developed to the point of providing the proper training for citizenship. If colleges and universities were not to change their curricula to permit an examination of the philosophy underlying American society, Meiklejohn feared that ignorance would characterize all basic political decisions. He did not want the curriculum to deal with matters of operational utility, nor did he want the college itself to become involved in practical affairs. An understanding of contemporary philosophical assumptions was crucial. All citizens had to understand those assumptions if a cohesive community was to exist. Without such a community, prejudice and violence instead of discussion would determine the future of the United States.

As he viewed America, he concluded that colleges and universities were failing to produce enough properly educated graduates. Hence America was drifting away from reason toward blind acceptance of governmental policy and action. During the 1920's, the 1930's, and the McCarthy era, he decried the failure of the people to exercise their Constitutional obligation to control their government. They were allowing the government, supposedly their agent, to dictate to them. In his opinion, the country was witnessing the mere perpetuation of established patterns rather than the initiation of new ideas.

He shared the negative view of Babbitt, Nock, Flexner, and Hutchins about the political understanding of the American people. Public opinion, he stated, exists little above that of a mob which feels but does not think, which does not judge but follows changing impulse and caprice. He condemned the mental processes of the ordinary voter and legislator as intellectually "quite disreputable."[5]

---

[5]Alexander Meiklejohn, *The Experimental College* (New York, 1932), pp. 167-168.

As Meiklejohn observed the condition of twentieth-century man and society, he lamented the state of American public opinion, for he believed that at no time in history had man needed more light upon great human affairs. Like Babbitt, Nock, Flexner, and Hutchins, he thought that the old Graeco-Christian civilization upon which America had been built was dying and that a new world, powerless to be born, awaited creation. The form which the new social order would take was not yet evident, and new patterns of social intelligence had to arise to mold the new society.

Meiklejohn called for the people to educate themselves so they could consciously control their society. The destiny of America, he wrote

rests upon the issue as to whether or not we can find ways of setting up over against our material activity an intellectual and moral and aesthetic insight, free enough and powerful enough to direct it whither we will that it shall go.[6]

This education did not involve a concentration upon techniques to facilitate greater operating ability within current societal institutions. Meiklejohn's concept of education for intelligence meant rather a study of the basic assumptions of the American system.

AMERICAN COLLEGES FOR INTELLIGENCE

Meiklejohn defined liberal education as the cultivation of powers enabling citizens to order their relations with themselves, their fellows, and the world. Hence by definition liberal education offered the solution to the ordering of a democracy. Meiklejohn believed that if every citizen could receive a liberal education, a true democratic social order could come into being. He once defined democracy as "a society whose citizens

---

[6]Alexander Meiklejohn, "Educational Leadership in America," *Harper's Magazine,* CLX (1930), 447.

are liberally educated."[7] In fact, America could approach a democratic society only to the extent that it approached universal liberal education. Reflecting a basic adherence to Rousseau's political philosophy, he therefore advocated state action, if necessary, to force people to be educated. Men in a democracy should not be free merely to think. They must think well, especially about matters basic to their control of society.

Therefore, Meiklejohn wanted everyone to receive a liberal education which was to begin immediately after the completion of high school. He thought that the understanding necessary for the creation of an intelligent electorate could be developed then. After his Wisconsin experiment, he thought that two years of liberal education would be enough for everyone, but he never explicitly proposed the establishment of two-year liberal colleges for the whole country.

Meiklejohn admitted that students needed vocational training. He simply did not think that such education belonged in college. Vocational training would not provide the basic insight necessary for fundamental political decisions.

As against the immediate practical demands from without, the issue is clear and decisive. College teachers know that the world must have trained workmen, skilled operatives, clever buyers and sellers, efficient directors, resourceful manufacturers, able lawyers, ministers, physicians, and teachers. But it is equally true that in order to do its own work, the liberal college must leave the special and technical training for these trades and professions to be done in other schools and by other methods. In a word, the liberal college does not pretend to give all the kinds of teaching which a young man of college age may profitably receive; it does not even claim to give all the kinds of intellectual training which are

---

[7]Alexander Meiklejohn, "The Future of Liberal Education," *New Republic*, Jan. 25, 1943, p. 115.

worth giving. It is committed to intellectual training of the liberal type.[8]

Vocational education, an important part of the concept of higher education for operational utility, simply did not appeal to Meiklejohn as the best means to equip the student for controlling his society. It resulted more from the materialistic values which Meiklejohn feared were tearing asunder the American community. Greater understanding of the principles of the American community, not greater vocational abilities, was to result from Meiklejohn's college.

Throughout all his writings runs an antipathy toward materialistic values. He condemned the honor which they received in America and lamented that the college had to cater to them. In his opinion no person should confuse education with the desire for so-called success in what he considered the distorted, materialistic American scheme of values. The art of understanding one's own life and that of the community does not result from vocational education.

He never drafted specific proposals for state-controlled liberal education because he was not certain that a definitive answer existed for the question of what courses constituted a liberal education. He agreed with Hutchins that the great books of Western civilization touch upon all phases of human experience, and he thought that the person who had read them might well become familiar with all fields of experience. This familiarity might give him the ability to react to any situation with a background of experience. He was not, however, sure that the great books would necessarily result in social intelligence. This uncertainty explains his interest in educational experimentation. He established the Wisconsin Experimental College in 1928, for example, to test some of his ideas in the hope that evidence could be gathered for establishing curricular requirements.

---

[8]Alexander Meiklejohn, "The Aim of the Liberal College," in Maurice G. Fulton, ed., *College Life* (New York, 1921), pp. 34-35.

At Wisconsin he tried to see whether or not students could grasp the essential characteristics of American society in two years of study. He enrolled about seventy students each year. During the freshman year all of them read some of the great writers of ancient Greece such as Homer, Herodotus, Thucydides, Sophocles, Plato, and Aristotle. During the sophomore year everyone read some of the great American authors including Henry Adams, Walt Whitman, Henry George, Thorstein Veblen, and Walter Lippmann. The contrast between the two cultures was to highlight the major trends of both.

Classwork was kept informal and instruction was carried on in small discussion groups. Students were required to write critical essays dealing with topics like the life of Euripides, industrial problems in Wheeling, West Virginia, and the function and value of art. Since students had one-fourth of their time free to take electives in the University of Wisconsin proper, they would have an opportunity to study mathematics or languages, which they would need in order to complete a regular academic major during their junior and senior years.

At the end of the experiment in 1933, Meiklejohn thought that his students had a good grasp of the main characteristics of American society and hence had received a liberal education. Therefore, when he established his School of Social Studies in San Francisco, he adopted essentially the same course of readings, but after the School was discontinued he changed his mind.

Shortly before he died in 1964, he stated that a curriculum built around the decisions of the United States Supreme Court might well provide the best opportunity for young people to develop their intelligence.[9] Since the stresses of American society can be traced in these decisions perhaps better than in any other writings, the student would be familiar with the major forces of the society in which he lived. Even this proposal,

---

[9]Interview with author.

however, would have had to be tested before Meiklejohn would have recommended its general adoption. His advocacy of experimentation in higher education thus continued to his death.

Collegiate Detachment from Society

During his long life devoted to education, Meiklejohn reiterated that intelligence consisted of the power to control one's environment. Oddly enough, for a person holding this position, he never advocated the scholarly study of the detailed functioning of American social, political, and economic life. Instead he called upon the world of scholarship to search for the philosophical understanding men need to rule wisely. He rejected the gathering of facts upon which useful concepts must rest. Instead, he favored a deductive approach dealing with philosophical concepts without major attention to the socio-political order. This sets him apart from the advocates of general education for operational utility.

Although Meiklejohn wanted liberal education to provide the link between the world of the scholar and that of practice, he opposed the utilitarian notion of professorial involvement in social problems. The academic man must only be committed to the development of his students' intelligence. Meiklejohn admitted that teaching has to spring from a vital interest in fundamental problems of human life or it will become a pithless thing, but he did not advocate faculty participation in the world of affairs.

Men as they act must choose between conflicting thoughts; and as the differing thoughts form differing groups, these get committed to their points of view; and action ever tends to harden thoughts into convictions, dogmas, and prejudices, to make men feel that in themselves thinking has reached its goal. Meanwhile the teacher stands apart, viewing the process as a whole. His faith is not in any party or its doctrines. His faith is in the mind of man. He teaches younger people

*to be men—in thinking. If he can reach that end, then he
has done his work.*[10]

In other words, scholars and teachers have an obligation to
think freely, and in his opinion they cannot do this if they
participate in social action. They would then become partisan
themselves. If the colleges and universities or their professors
become involved in partisan issues, Meiklejohn predicted that
they will cease to be institutions where truth is sought and where
thought is free.

He actually feared that professorial involvement in politics
might draw colleges and universities into what he called the
one genuine pedagogic sin: dragging students to preconceived
conclusions while pretending to lead them to the truth.[11]
Professionally the teacher does not "train for any party, any
creed, nor, in the deepest sense, for any nation."[12] The teacher
should develop in his students the ability to do their own thinking, not to accept on blind faith what he tells them.

Meiklejohn admitted that the purpose of all teaching *"is to
express the cultural authority of the group by which the teaching is given."*[13] He held that in America, however, the prevailing democratic culture depended not upon indoctrination but
instead upon the rigorous development of the will and the
capacity for independent judgment in the youth. The very
idea of indoctrinating Americanism was inimical to Meiklejohn's notion of American ideals, as it was to most educational
thinkers of his day.

Agreeing with Babbitt, Nock, Flexner, and Hutchins,
Meiklejohn thought that scholars would serve their age and

---

[10]Alexander Meiklejohn, "The College and the Common Life," *Harper's
Magazine*, CXLVII (1923) , 726.

[11]Alexander Meiklejohn, "Freedom of the College," *Atlantic Monthly*,
CXXI (1918) , 87.

[12]Meiklejohn, "The College and the Common Life," p. 726.

[13]Meiklejohn, *Education Between Two Worlds*, p. 91.

circumstance by training students to think critically for themselves. They would thus check the popular drift of ideas. Specific instruction dealing with the techniques and details of society's ills were of little worth. Broad questions related to the general social scheme, he held, would stimulate students to think incisively about the problems hindering the progress of society. By molding human beings in this manner, he maintained, the liberal college can fight the forces of inhumanity and can work toward the creation of a political order in which humane ends dominate over ends destructive of man.

Meiklejohn thus envisioned the liberal college as a means of renewing civilization, but not, like the Wisconsin progressives, as a device for direct action itself. He compared colleges to the nerve centers in an organism: not large in bulk, not self-sufficient, not adequate for action in the outside world—yet in charge of action. Colleges are in charge of action because they mold the minds which will later decide what society will do. In effect, Meiklejohn asserted, the colleges should not assume any social responsibility other than that of making the minds which will run society.

> *Out of the quiet little places where men and boys assemble for study of human life and of the world—out of those places has shone forth a light which illumined human life, which has made clearer the world in which we live. . . . Men everywhere are making human life, are making mankind to be a stronger, finer thing than it has been. And in the doing of that task, they choose to set aside some quiet groups for Making Minds. Those groups are Liberal Colleges.*[14]

Favoring higher education for all young Americans, Meiklejohn thought that the colleges, isolated from the cares of the practical world, could revolutionize the style of thinking of the entire electorate.

---

[14]Alexander Meiklejohn, *The Liberal College* (Boston, 1920), p. 9.

Disruptive Influences Upon American Colleges

Nothing is more clear than that, taken as a whole, the present attempt of our schools and colleges to establish our young people in the ways of sensitiveness and intelligence is a ludicrous failure. . . . They are not made ready to play their part in the life of a democracy.[15]

According to Meiklejohn, colleges lacked not only an understanding of the human situation upon which the instruction of a democratic people should be based, but also any effective method for developing the social intelligence of the students. Unfortunately, he observed, colleges did not appear about to change, for they did not possess any sense of experimentation to find a way out of their predicament.

A rather polite, widespread fear of upsetting contemporary academic traditions, Meiklejohn asserted, made reform of the college almost out of the question. His own troubles at Wisconsin, where the regular university faculty ridiculed his Experimental College because of its supposed dilettantism, convinced him that bigotry within higher education itself could wreck hopes for reform. Although he realized that his faculty did not possess the academic qualifications to teach courses dealing with both Greek and American civilizations, he believed that the University had no valid basis for discontinuing his experiment. Professorial prejudice would always arise against educational ventures outside the purview of established academic disciplines.

The influence of the outside environment upon higher education made his situation even worse. Unlike Flexner, Meiklejohn could not find in society the intellectual and cultural purpose needed to provide the desired content and direction to the college. He realized that the strength of the discipline of the college upon its students had to lie in the fact that the values of the college represent powerful forces in the

---

[15]Alexander Meiklejohn, *What Does America Mean?* (New York, 1935), p. 234.

community and are recognized as such by the person being disciplined. If citizens as a whole do not hold the conviction that intelligence is necessary, its support by the academic world will lack the touch of needed reality. In viewing the nation, he feared that the nonacademic world was not providing the proper direction for the American college. The country was not educating her children because Meiklejohn's contemporaries were not educated themselves.

His disdain of both faculty and general social opinion probably accounts for his failure to initiate lasting reforms in American higher education. At Amherst his bald confrontation with what became a majority of the faculty cost him the presidency. At Wisconsin his failure again to convince academic men of the wisdom of his venture resulted in the destruction of his experiment. Finally, in San Francisco his miscalculation of public support eventuated in the collapse of his school.

Changes Needed Within the Colleges

Although Meiklejohn did not want professors to be engaged in the solution of practical problems, he thought that the first prerequisite for a decent college was faculty members whom the community recognized as its intellectual leaders. "No man who cannot lead his peers is fit to teach the younger generation."[16] From his experience with professors, Meiklejohn thought that they lacked the intellectual qualities and leadership requisite to their callings. He stated that most of them were really uneducated. They failed to grasp the significance of human experience. By no stretch of the imagination could he imagine a college faculty being recognized by most people as the guide for their thinking.

In order to improve the educational potential of the professoriate, he wanted colleges to develop their own sense of

---

16Meiklejohn, "Freedom of the College," p. 86.

intellectual community. If members of the faculty could know each other not just socially, but professionally, he believed they could carry on much better intellectual work. For this reason, like Nock, he advised limiting the enrollment of each college to two hundred fifty students and twenty teachers.

Further, he advocated the abolition of academic departments. In his own endeavors, Meiklejohn put considerable effort into attempts to develop a curriculum independent of the limits imposed by departments. At Wisconsin he had not allowed departments, and his experience convinced him that knowledge should not be segmented into academic disciplines. He wanted the president to work for unity and understanding within the institution. He then envisioned students and faculty becoming an intellectual community devoted to understanding the world. His two-year program focusing only on the great books of the Greek and American civilizations certainly did not fall within the traditional departments. He simply wanted students to search for the patterns within their culture.[17] At Amherst his favored course in social science integrated work from various disciplines. Unrelated courses, in his opinion, could not effectively result in intelligence.

As already mentioned, Meiklejohn never claimed to have found the definitive curriculum. He in fact came to believe that its actual content was unimportant, as long as it dealt with man. Since Meiklejohn believed that the student should be able to think intelligently about his social environment, he thought that training in mathematics or classics was nonessential. Even the little work in the natural sciences which he included in the Wisconsin Experimental College related to man's use of nature rather than to nature itself. In short, Meiklejohn believed that the task of the college lies in opening to the student the content of human life. It should arouse his

---

[17]Alexander Meiklejohn, "The Unity of the Curriculum," *New Republic*, supplement, Oct. 25, 1922, p. 3.

interests in the riches of human experience—literature, nature, art, religion, philosophy, politics, and the other areas of learning which can raise the quality of subjective, nonoperational human existence.

He emphasized that the college should never forget that it does not bear its prime obligation to truth and knowledge but to "the people who need the truth."[18]   In this sense, he differed sharply with Flexner who urged a concentration upon truth and knowledge, not people.   In Meiklejohn's mind, the only legitimate purpose of the American college lay in the development of the power and zest for intelligent participation in the decisions of a democratic society. Meiklejohn would have judged the results of college training not in terms of what scholars do, as Flexner suggested, but rather in terms of the thought and actions of its graduates in the ordinary relations of life.

Education for Social Intelligence

In summation, Meiklejohn's reasons for opposing educational operational utility differ from those of Babbitt, Nock, Flexner, and Hutchins. He, more than any of them, recognized the need for coming to grips with the practical problems of twentieth-century society through general education. He was concerned, for instance, with the kinds of problems which the Supreme Court considered. Yet he did not want colleges and universities to serve as institutions of operational utility. Perhaps the following quotation indicates in brief his feelings about direct involvement:

> *To serve one's fellows, to play one's part in the social scheme is, we presume, to substitute better living for worse, finer for coarser, worth while for less worth while. But how shall one do this unless he know what living is, know it through and through so that he may lead, not as one who is blind, but as one who has seen the light. Too often, it seems to me, those of us who go out to help our fellows to live have little*

---

[18]Meiklejohn, "Teaching of Intellectual Freedom," p. 15.

conception of what kind of life is worth living, and so we fall into the blind mechanism of the things that are taken for granted, and we give them roads and bridges, motor cars and battleships, shorter hours and larger pay without ever a question whether these are the ways in which men can best be brought to the successful practice of the art of living. Surely it is true that the college must send its students out to serve, but it must first open their eyes and give them a vision which they may carry with them as the guide and inspiration of their work.[19]

Thus he approved the basic purpose behind higher education for operational utility, but he criticized it for concentrating upon operational technique to the neglect of basic philosophical understanding. He wanted his college to concentrate upon

the value of knowledge: not the specialized knowledge which contributes to immediate practical aims, but the unified understanding which is Insight.[20]

Meiklejohn clearly did not want the college to be of operational utility to society. He did not like professorial involvement in social problems; he did not want vocational education included in his curriculum; and his proposals for the study of Greek and American civilization made obvious his feelings about operational utility in general education.

Like the other critics of higher education for operational utility, Meiklejohn wanted the college to be an ivory tower separated from the vicissitudes of contemporary life. Although at Amherst he at one time encouraged a program to involve students in the operational concerns of the area, he did not think that a college should become confused with operational details. They would deflect the college from its primary purpose: the development of social intelligence.

---

[19]Alexander Meiklejohn, "College Education and the Moral Ideal," *Education*, XXVIII (1908), 561.

[20]Meiklejohn, "Aim of the Liberal College," p. 52.

In his writings, Meiklejohn focused upon problems of the college. He did not write extensively about university education or the role of other institutions of higher learning. He did not deal with research and its place in colleges and universities, and he did not decry extension services. He simply worried about the failure of colleges to provide liberal education. Society's concentration upon materialistic goals was subverting the philosophical understanding which Meiklejohn believed necessary for a democratic community. He wanted colleges to be established which could educate students liberally. Other institutions of higher learning might well serve the operational needs of society, but strong liberal colleges were necessary if the country was to become strongly democratic.

When Meiklejohn admitted the necessity of creating an intelligent society before intelligent people can develop, he revealed the basically sentimental nature of his thought. What is a society other than the sum of the people who comprise it? If one admits that the social environment must be rationally ordered before colleges can be constructed intelligently, what is the pioneering role of higher education? It would become merely an agent for moving the young into the existing social order. Meiklejohn's thought, then, is essentially tautological. A better society will result from better colleges, but better colleges will not emerge until a better society exists. He should have emphasized the long process of interaction between colleges and society in the course of their mutual growth.

More centrally, Meiklejohn should have dealt with the question of why intelligence, defined simply as conscious control of one's human environment, would necessarily result in the exaltation of human life. He assumed that men who know what they are doing will act in the best interest of all. If he had met Babbitt or Nock, they might well have informed him that men, acting consciously, can harm as well as help others. The example of Nazi Germany, where men consciously controlled society for the purposes of radical evil, should have brought this question into Meiklejohn's writings.

In spite of these weaknesses, one central message lies in Meiklejohn's thought which American colleges and universities should note: namely, that somewhere in the world of scholarship a place is needed where the diverse and scattered findings of modern research can be integrated and focused upon the common life of society. Unfortunately, he did not question why this sort of integrated knowledge could not be compatible with knowledge of direct operational utility. He did not even deal with the issue.

Nor did he discuss how a person could control himself or his environment without a knowledge of the operational techniques of control. Control entails mastery of the methods of execution as well as the determination of policy. Meiklejohn dealt only with policy and not with means. A systematic, disciplined thinker would not have made that mistake.

Meiklejohn's personal stand for social and educational objectives leaves little doubt about his sincerity regarding the value of certain goals. His difficulties in reaching his objectives, however, reveal his romanticism regarding the means of implementing those ends. The same flaw marked his life as that which marks his thought.

CHAPTER EIGHT

CONCLUSION:
The Social Relevance of Higher Education

The issue is not between practical and intellectual aims but between the immediate and the remote aim, between the hasty and the measured procedure, between the demand for results at once and the willingness to wait for the best results.

ALEXANDER MEIKLEJOHN, 1921

ONE MIGHT LOGICALLY ASK: Did the critics of higher education for operational utility really say anything of significance? Were they truly counterrevolutionary and representing traditions which were being pushed aside and which needed a rationale, indeed any rationale, to justify their continuation? Were all of them serious in their assertions that universities and colleges for operational utility were accelerating the decay of Western civilization? Were their ideas relevant to the future of the nation?

Although Babbitt, Nock, Flexner, Hutchins, and Meiklejohn rejected the premises of the ideal of operational utility for higher education, they all expected colleges and universities to relate to the problems of society. Each simply differed with the leaders of American higher education regarding the priority of those problems. Opposing the notion that the country's real needs were operational in nature, each of them believed that they were more fundamental.

Babbitt distrusted the very assumptions of American democracy. Fearing that most men could never control their lust for material and physical satisfactions, he thought that higher education must concentrate on the creation and transmission to an elite of cultural controls which could substitute for the restraints characteristic of the Graeco-Christian tradition. Nock's position in some degree paralleled Babbitt's, for his formative knowledge concerned the cultivation of the Remnant, not the training of the Masses in operational techniques. Flexner opposed higher education for operational utility primarily because he thought that it would not produce the conceptual research needed for the progress of civilization. Hutchins lamented with Flexner that colleges and universities were in fact a mirror of their society rather than a beacon to it. Institutions of higher learning had to discover metaphysical principles and transmit them to all the people, or American democracy was doomed. Like Hutchins, Meiklejohn thought that colleges should drop their concern for matters of operational utility because they did not touch the basic problems of democracy. An understanding of the philosophical assumptions of a modern, industrial democracy by the student was to him the most crucial goal for American higher education.

In short, then, each of these five men stated that his ideas were far more relevant to the modern age than those of the advocates of operational utility. Given the views about man and society upon which each of them based his educational thought, each was logical in calling for a separation of colleges and universities from the operational needs of society. Each had just cause to fear the impact of higher education for operational utility upon his respective ideals. The soundness of their assumptions and thus their goals for higher education, however, remains an open question.

In an age of automation, America now has the resources to support at least some of the educational institutions which either Babbitt, Nock, Flexner, Hutchins, or Meiklejohn favored.

To suggest that all colleges and universities follow one of their plans, however, is another matter. Their proposals rest upon assumptions which neglect the everyday functioning of society, and only a romantic would expect society to allow the implementation of any of their educational ideals as the dominant pattern for American higher education. Perhaps in this regard Nock was the most realistic of the five, for he recognized the impossibility of transforming his ideas into reality.

These five men failed to meet the demands of their environment. Most people around them were not in fact receptive to their proposals. Those individuals and groups capable of financing the nation's colleges or universities thought the ideas of these men irrelevant to their needs. Without the backing of trustees and legislators, no one could make major changes in American colleges and universities. Those people in control of wealth, both public and private, wanted colleges and universities to be responsive to their operational needs. They did not want colleges and universities to upset the status quo. Babbitt, Nock, Flexner, Hutchins, and Meiklejohn failed to meet this financial question directly. Instead they all continued to call for a restructuring of higher education counter to the whole societal framework. Thus their ideas had little chance of being institutionalized, and in fact the exhortations of these five men have not substantially altered the practices of American colleges and universities.

The ideal of operational utility for colleges and universities has proven too attractive for a dynamic, industrial country. Those wielding power in America value the general education, the vocational training, the research, the extension courses, and the professorial advice of the operationally oriented colleges and universities too much to change them from fear of some general cultural disintegration. Culture is an elusive thing. The complex of contemporary and traditional ideas and achievements which constitute a culture often are not clear to even the most perceptive observer. On the other hand, specific operational needs give rise to definite demands obvious to state legislators and private donors. Since those responsible for the policy of American higher education must remain responsive to their sources of financial income, they must cater to the wishes of those who can furnish them money, or their colleges and universities will perish. Thus, although the rich diversity of American higher education testifies to the rather divergent wishes of various interest groups and individuals, colleges and universities have still had to remain rather responsive to nonacademic groups concerned with the operational utility of knowledge.

The ideas of these five critics are not significant for the impact they have had upon the orientation of colleges and universities toward operational utility, for as yet they have made no extensive impression. True, innovations at the University of Chicago, Amherst College, the Wisconsin Experimental College, the San Francisco School of Social Studies, the St. John's Colleges, the Center for the Study of Democratic Institutions, and the Institute for Advanced Study at Princeton provide evidence that these five men did affect higher education to some degree. Undoubtedly their ideas further stimulated discussions on countless other campuses across the land. Yet the practices of most of the country's more than 2,400 institutions of higher education have remained largely unchanged by the criticism levied by the five counterrevolutionists.

Admittedly, movements in the 1960's toward clusters of colleges, smaller residential units, expanded honors programs, and extended foreign study opportunities represent efforts to meliorate some of the same problems which these five critics discerned. These latest innovations, however, have largely not been made by men motivated by their opposition to the operational utility of higher education. These five men appear somewhat irrelevant to these new features.

Furthermore, other developments in American higher education made many of the proposals of these five critics largely irrelevant. The staggering increase in the number of students enrolled in colleges and universities would have made most difficult the implementation of the education for limited numbers of students favored by Babbitt, Nock, and Flexner. In 1880 when all three of them were young, only slightly more than two percent of the population between the ages of eighteen and twenty-one were enrolled in college. In absolute figures this represents about 68,000 students. Shortly after Nock's death, however, this percentage had not only increased to over twenty percent, but the actual number had burgeoned to over 2,600,000. Today more than 7,000,000 students are enrolled.

The enormous problems involved in providing not only the physical facilities but also the faculty for these numbers would have made planning on the scale envisioned by them most difficult. The plans of Babbitt, Nock, and Flexner made no provision for the millions who wanted to flock to a college or university. In a basically democratic nation, the probability of the electorate accepting their dictum epitomized by Nock's proposal that all but the geniuses be dumped on the "rubbish heap" appears absurd. The notion of a literary Remnant guiding American society is divorced from reality. If the nation were to respond to any educated elite, it would probably respond to an elite gifted with knowledge of operational utility.

Of equal difficulty for the implementation of the plans of Babbitt, Nock, Hutchins, and Meiklejohn was the problem of educating a professoriate capable of staffing the new kinds of institutions which they envisioned. Could enough people assimilate the material required to teach their curricula? Mastery of the techniques for perceiving cultural standards, formative knowledge, metaphysical principles, or social intelligence does not come quickly, if at all.

The conflict between teaching and research alone would have made difficult the attainment of the academic goals of all these five men except Flexner. Since the 1890's the academic profession has relied progressively more for prestige upon esoteric factual research than upon teaching. In spite of some small programs now being established to train college teachers instead of research scholars, those who oppose graduate education for research have not been able to make serious headway.

Only Flexner's idea of research would have fit into the academic world's present value structure. Babbitt approved of research in a university solely when it related to the creation of cultural standards. Nock considered research irrelevant to the crucial issues in American higher education. Hutchins disapproved of all academic research unrelated to metaphysical principles. Meiklejohn wanted broad philosophical training for future college teachers. Thus the graduate schools were simply not going to prepare the kind of teachers these four men desired. In fact, the training in esoteric fields demanded in nearly all Ph.D. programs was the reverse of what Babbitt, Nock, Hutchins, and Meiklejohn believed crucial.

Flexner's conception of the role of graduate education would also have run counter to strong tendencies in American education. Although in 1900 only 342 Ph.D. degrees were awarded, by 1950 this figure had risen to more than 10,000. Today even that figure has roughly tripled. By no means could the Institute for Advanced Study or other similar institutions have produced these numbers. The alternative, fewer colleges for fewer students, might have made his proposal partially tenable, but even then no provision would have existed for the preparation of instructors for the technically able persons who were to be trained in operationally oriented schools beyond the limits of colleges and universities.

Those responsible for shaping educational policy during the great revolution in higher education during the latter part of the nineteenth century largely rejected the notion that vocational training should be placed in institutions apart from nonvocational education. Thus strictly vocational programs were included in the same schools as the traditional academic subjects. The Land-Grant College Act of 1862 specifically required that the mechanical and agricultural arts accompany other scientific and classical studies in the institutions receiving funds through it. Twentieth-century leaders in higher education have actively extended this principle.

The democratic ethos demanded collegiate social standing for farmers and technicians. Large segments of the population simply wanted colleges and universities to provide a social experience for young people which would enhance their ability to operate in certain social spheres. Frederick Jackson Turner pointed out that colleges and universities might well be the safety valve for society after the closing of the frontier. Regardless of the validity of his assertion, many students and parents probably look upon college years more as a means of making the right contacts and acquiring the social skills supposedly characteristic of college graduates than of mastering any kind of classroom knowledge, operational or not.[1] In a mobile society lacking many of the traditional status considerations of class-stratified societies, the college degree represents one of the few definite assurances of one's social acceptability. People interested in higher education for this variety of social utility really do not care what collegiate academic programs offer, as long as the outward characteristics of college life become imprinted upon the young.

In light of these considerations, severe attempts to restrict enrollment would probably have caused bitter public animosity toward colleges and universities. Hutchins and Meiklejohn were probably wiser observers of American society than Babbitt, Nock, and Flexner in this regard, for they clearly wanted a college education for everyone. Most Americans, however, cared little about either Hutchins' intellectual power or Meiklejohn's

---

[1]See Elizabeth Douvan and Carol Kaye, "Motivational Factors in College Entrance," in Nevitt Sanford, ed., *The American College* (New York, 1962), pp. 199-224.

social intelligence. What could be further from the popular mentality than such ideas?

To complicate the wishes of all five even more, the competition between the United States and the Soviet Union after World War II has forced colleges and universities to adjust to a semi-mobilized war-state. Many faculty and students alike resent the university's orientation toward the operational requirements of industry and the military during this time of trial, but the state exerts immense force upon colleges and universities to serve the national interest. In a time when technology and the operating efficiency of society make the difference between national defeat and national triumph, pressures for colleges and universities to become institutions of direct operational utility become almost overwhelming.

The Cold War, however, has merely heightened the necessity for training the professional men required by modern society. Even in peacetime, America needs men who can manage the complexities of her socioeconomic order. All of the critics except Flexner relied upon education of an essentially literary nature. Babbitt, Nock, Hutchins, and Meiklejohn treated as nonessential the education needed for a scientific, industrial society to function. Proudly, they displayed their disdain for scientific and technological education. This rejection of the basis of contemporary society was damning.

All four of them had to admit that such education should be offered by some institution other than colleges or universities. They simply did not think it important enough to elaborate upon its proper nature. The advocates of operational utility had been wonderful at outlining how society should attain its goals, but they were helpless in determining what those goals should be. Babbitt, Nock, Flexner, Hutchins, and Meiklejohn, on the other hand, wrote considerably about those goals, but they had no effective method for implementing them.

Even on the purely intellectual level, they failed to confront directly the forces they opposed. With the exception of Flexner, they all denounced pragmatism. Yet pragmatism, perhaps the leading American philosophy of the twentieth century, in fact enveloped their ideas. Not only Babbitt but also Hutchins and Meiklejohn defined the standards which they would establish in terms of the laws of man's nature. They admitted that these laws were evidenced in what men did and in fact were definable in terms of men's actions over a long period of time. Therefore, James' pragmatism, taken simply as being that doctrine which judges a proposition by its workability, would correspond well with their definitions. Standards, the three of them would have agreed, come from observations of men's deeds, and man can himself discern these standards. James would not have disagreed with such a position. Standards based upon observable experience do not reflect formalism but pragmatic liberalism or pragmatic conservatism.

At the root of all their criticism lay the fear that Western culture would disintegrate if colleges and universities did not produce nonutilitarian knowledge and educate the young to understand and respect it, irrespective of its relation to the immediate cares of society. To one degree or another, pragmatism and its allies, instrumentalism and legal realism, therefore drew the wrath of all these critics. In opposing colleges and universities of operational utility to society, all five asserted that the focus of higher education upon operational matters denies that truths exist above the changing nature of contemporary needs. Unless colleges and universities recognized their independence from the operational problems of society, men with concern only for technique and facilitation would graduate from them. Likewise the knowledge produced by colleges and universities would be devoid of value for the establishment of a better society. They feared a rather complete interest in means to the exclusion of lasting principles.

Certainly, in any civilization worthy of the name, nonoperational values which lead to a standard of living above the purely animal and material are necessary. Man's spiritual, aesthetic, and moral needs require satisfaction. Serious students of American culture, these critics perceived a shift among thinking people from values long cherished by members of traditional Western society. Immediately involved in colleges and universities themselves, they recognized that a complex, modern nation must rely upon formal education to prepare the young for participation in its culture. They thought that the basic cultural problems of America required the primary attention of colleges and universities, and as they realized, these fundamental issues indeed deserve attention.

With new means of industrial production already coming into being, a new life awaits mankind in developed countries. Most men must no longer spend the majority of their waking hours struggling for mere material survival. Colleges and universities must not shun the confrontation with this new day. They must educate men to live whole lives, both within society and by themselves. Man is indeed more than an instrument of use to others and himself. The tendency to specialize man into a highly refined tool can dehumanize him and make him little more than a machine. Colleges and universities should give recognition by their practices that man's rational, artistic, and spiritual potential all need development.

With the increasing importance of specialized knowledge in the functioning of American society, colleges and universities, and especially major research universities, are becoming the major institutions responsible for the continuation and advancement of society. They are not only in the mainstream of American life, they are perhaps becoming the major current in that stream. This is good, too, for it keeps colleges and universities in vital touch with life and keeps them financially strong. They should use their considerable influence to work for a society of good values as well as one of great operating expertise.

A central consideration of this book is the question: What kind of education can the current American social structure be expected to support? Americans have always had somewhat ambivalent feelings about the value of formal higher education. In the middle of the nineteenth century, as pointed out previously, both the percentage and actual number of students attending colleges and universities declined, indicating a widespread lack of confidence in the worth of a college education. Formal higher education did not begin to regain popular esteem until the initial impact of the Land-Grant College Act in the 1870's. Since that time it has been adjusting to the operational concerns of society.

In Congress in the late twentieth century, financial aid for colleges and universities must for the most part be argued on the basis of national defense. At the time of this writing, with the exception of grants intended for minority group students, most undergraduate federal scholarships, for instance, are related in some fashion to national defense. Within recent years general grants for buildings and guaranteed bank loans for students have become available, but if higher education were only to result in the production of knowledge of high cultural value and men of integrity, the representatives of the American people might well refuse to assist it without the prodding of the Cold War.

Nevertheless, literate America has consistently placed its faith in its colleges and universities. Perhaps, however, this faith never lay with the nonoperational literary values characteristic of the nineteenth-century American college. Francis Wayland, the distinguished president of Brown, indicated as much in his penetrating analysis of American higher education published in 1842.[2] He stated that colleges and universities could survive only if they concentrated their energies upon the solution of practical economic and technological problems.

---

[2]Francis Wayland, *Thoughts on the Present Collegiate System in the United States* (Boston, 1842).

Our five counterrevolutionists disagreed vigorously with Wayland's central assertion. With the exception of Nock, all of them began their careers with a strong, optimistic faith that a first-rate college or university education of no operational utility could command enough support to enable its survival. Babbitt and Flexner never lost this commitment, but Hutchins and Meiklejohn did. They never drifted as far as Nock by denying the total possibility of establishing the right kind of colleges and universities, but they seriously doubted it. Hutchins, after his failure at Chicago, and Meiklejohn, after his at Wisconsin, both turned to the field of adult education because they realized that colleges and universities cannot change significantly in the face of overwhelming unfavorable public opinion. Flexner likewise moved into an educational institution removed from direct work with college students. The Institute for Advanced Study resembles one of the academies of the eighteenth century more closely than it does one of the German universities of the nineteenth.

Perhaps basic American anti-intellectualism accounts for the disillusionment which the critics of the concept of operational utility in higher education came to feel. America values intellect, to be sure, but primarily when intellect can offer material testimony of its worth. The leaders of the new American universities in the late nineteenth century realized this and therefore, unlike Babbitt, Nock, Flexner, Hutchins, and Meiklejohn, achieved their goals for higher education. The men examined in this study did not realize their objectives within the American system of colleges and universities because they did not understand America's value of intellect.

Yet in a new age when operational demands have changed, many proposals of these men take on new relevance. The issues which they discussed are by no means dead, and renewed, dynamic colleges and universities may well find good reason to turn to the principles of these critics of operational utility. America values material objectives, but strong idealistic strains appear within American history. In an age materially secure, the nonoperational values characteristic of American colleges before the revolution in nineteenth-century higher education may well appear relevant to society's leaders. No country, any more than any individual, can find fulfillment in land and gold alone. Culture involves far more, and the future of the nation, indeed of civilization, lies in its response to nonmaterial as well as material challenges.

BIBLIOGRAPHY

I. GENERAL MATERIALS

A. Higher Education: History and Perspectives

Barzun, Jacques. *The American University.* New York, 1968.

Beesley, Patricia. *The Revival of the Humanities in American Education.* New York, 1940.

Bell, Daniel. *The Reforming of General Education.* New York, 1966.

Boller, Betty. "American Humanism and Post-War Higher Education." Unpublished doctoral dissertation, Harvard University, 1960.

Buckley, William F. *God and Man at Yale.* Chicago, 1951.

Butts, R. Freeman. *The College Charts Its Course.* New York, 1939.

Conant, James B. "The University and the State." *Journal of Higher Education,* XVIII (1947), 281-286.

Cowley, W. H. "Hamilton College Survey: The Curriculum." Unpublished, mimeographed, Hamilton College, 1940.

_____ "An Overview of American Colleges and Universities." Unpublished, mimeographed, Stanford University, 1960.

Cremin, Lawrence A. *The Transformation of the School.* New York, 1961.

Dewey, John. "The Problem of the Liberal Arts College." *American Scholar,* XIII (1944), 391-393.

Harvard University Faculty of Arts and Sciences, Committee of. *General Education in a Free Society.* Cambridge, 1945.

Hibbard, Addison. "The Revolution in College Educational Methods in America." *Current History,* XXX (1929), 387-395.

Hofstadter, Richard, and Walter P. Metzger. *The Development of Academic Freedom in the United States.* New York, 1955.

Hofstadter, Richard, and Wilson Smith. *American Higher Education: A Documentary History.* Chicago, 1961.

Hook, Sydney. *Education for Modern Man.* New York, 1946.

Huxley, Thomas H. *Science and Education.* New York, 1894.

Irsay, Stephen d'. *Histoire des universites francaises et etrangeres des origines a nos jours.* 2 vols. Paris, 1933-1935.

Jencks, Christopher, and David Riesman. *The Academic Revolution.* Garden City, 1968.

Jones, Howard Mumford. *Education and World Tragedy.* Cambridge, 1946.

Kerr, Clark. *The Uses of the University.* Cambridge, 1963.

Lilge, Friedrich. *The Abuse of Learning: the Failure of the German University.* New York, 1948.

McKeon, Richard. "Education and the Disciplines." *International Journal of Ethics,* XLVII (1937), 370-381.

Miller, Harry K., Jr. "A Study of the Field Service and Research Units of Ten Schools of Education." Unpublished doctoral dissertation, Stanford University, 1958.

Nevins, Allan. *The State Universities and Democracy.* Urbana, 1962.

Ornstein, Martha. *The Role of Scientific Societies in the Seventeenth Century.* Chicago, 1938.

Parsons, Talcott. "Remarks on Education and the Professions." *International Journal of Ethics,* XLVII (1937), 365-369.

Perry, Charner. "Education: Ideas or Knowledge?" *International Journal of Ethics,* XLVII (1937), 346-359.

Rashdall, Hastings. *The Universities of Europe in the Middle Ages.* New ed., 3 vols., Oxford, 1936.

Rudolph, Frederick. *The American College and University: A History.* New York, 1962.

Sanford, Nevitt, ed. *The American College: A Psychological and Social Interpretation of the Higher Learning.* New York, 1962.

Veblen, Thorstein. *The Higher Learning in America.* New York, 1957.

Veysey, Laurence R. *The Emergence of the American University.* Chicago, 1965.

Warren, W. Preston. "Philosophy, Politics, and Education: Our Basic Dilemma." *International Journal of Ethics,* XLVII (1937), 336-345.

Wayland, Francis. *Thoughts on the Present Collegiate System in the United States.* Boston, 1842.

Welter, Rush. *Popular Education and Democratic Thought in America.* New York, 1962.

Woodring, Paul. *The Higher Learning in America: A Reassessment.* New York, 1968.

Wright, Benjamin F., Jr. "History as a Central Study." *International Journal of Ethics,* XLVII (1937), 360-364.

B. The Intellectual in 20th Century America

Beale, Joseph H. "The World and the Scholar." *American Scholar,* I (1932), 50-57.

Cowley, Malcolm. *Exile's Return.* New York, 1956.

Curti, Merle, ed. *American Scholarship in the Twentieth Century.* Cambridge, 1953.

Hofstadter, Richard. *Anti-intellectualism in American Life.* New York, 1963.

Lippmann, Walter. "The Scholar in a Troubled World." *Atlantic Monthly,* CL (1932), 148-152.

Lipset, Seymour Martin. *Political Man: The Social Bases of Politics.* Garden City, 1963.

Merton, Robert K. "Role of the Intellectual in Public Bureaucracy." *Social Forces,* XXIII (1945), 405-415.

Michels, Roberto. "Intellectuals." *Encyclopedia of the Social Sciences,* VII, 118-126. New York, 1937.

Reid, Whitelaw. "The Scholar in Politics." *Scribner's Monthly,* VI (1873), 605-616.

Rogers, Lindsay. "University Professors in the Public Service." *Journal and Proceedings and Addresses of the 39th Annual Conference of the American Association of Universities,* XXXIX (1937), 94-97.

Shils, Edward. "The Intellectuals and the Powers." *Comparative Studies in Society and History,* I (1958), 5-22.

C. General Interpretive and Reference Material

Cargill, Oscar. *Intellectual America.* New York, 1948.

Commager, Henry Steele. *The American Mind.* New Haven, 1959.

Curti, Merle. *American Paradox: The Conflict of Thought and Action.* New Brunswick, 1956.

―――― *The Growth of American Thought.* New York, 1951.

Ekirch, Arthur A., Jr. *The American Democratic Tradition.* New York, 1963.

Frankel, Charles. *The Case for Modern Man.* Boston, 1960.

Gabriel, Ralph Henry. *The Course of American Democratic Thought.* New York, 1956.

Ginger, Ray. "The Idea of Progress in American Social Thought." *American Quarterly,* IV (1952), 253-265.

Hartz, Louis. *The Liberal Tradition in America.* New York, 1955.

Historical Statistics of the United States: Colonial Times to 1957. Washington, 1960.

Kazin, Alfred. *On Native Grounds.* New York, 1942.

May, Henry F. *The End of American Innocence.* New York, 1959.

―――― "Shifting Perspectives on the 1920's." *Mississippi Valley Historical Review,* XLIII (1956), 405-427.

Parrington, Vernon L. *Main Currents in American Thought.* Vol. III. New York, 1958.

Persons, Stow. *American Minds.* New York, 1958.

Potter, David M. *People of Plenty.* Chicago, 1954.

Rossiter, Clinton. *Conservatism in America.* New York, 1962.

Spitz, David. *Patterns of Anti-Democratic Thought.* New York, 1949.

White, Morton. *Social Thought in America: The Revolt Against Formalism.* Boston, 1957.

II. THE WISCONSIN IDEA

A. Primary Sources

Adams, Charles Kendall. *The Present Obligations of the Scholar: A Baccalaureate Address*. Madison, 1897.

_____ "The University and the State, Inaugural Address of President Adams." *The Addresses at the Inauguration of Charles Kendall Adams, LL.D. to the Presidency of the University of Wisconsin*. Madison, 1893.

Bascom, John. *Things Learned by Living*. New York and London, 1913.

Commons, John Rogers. "Constructive Investigation and the Industrial Commission of Wisconsin." *Survey,* Jan. 4, 1913, pp. 440-448.

_____ "Direct Legislation in Switzerland and America." *Arena,* XXII (1899), 725-739.

_____ "Discussion of the President's Address." American Economic Association, *Proceedings,* Third Series, I (1900), 62-80.

_____ *Eighteen Months' Work of the Milwaukee Bureau of Economy and Efficiency*. Milwaukee, 1912.

_____ "Is Class Conflict in America Growing and Is It Inevitable?" *American Journal of Sociology,* XIII (1908), 756-766.

_____ *Labor and Administration*. New York, 1913.

_____ *Legal Foundations of Capitalism*. New York, 1924.

_____ *Myself*. New York, 1934.

_____ "Progressive Individualism." *American Magazine of Civics,* VI (1895), 561-574.

_____ *Proportional Representation*. New York and Boston, 1896.

_____ "Referendum and Initiative in City Government." *Political Science Quarterly,* XVII (1902), 609-630.

_____ *Social Reform and the Church*. New York and Boston, 1894.

_____ "Three Meetings at New Orleans: The American Economic Association." *Review of Reviews,* XXIX (1904), 209-210.

Ely, Richard Theodore. "American Colleges and German Universities." *Harper's Monthly,* LXI (1880), 253-260.

_____ "Competition: Its Nature, Its Permanency and Its Beneficence." American Economic Association, *Proceedings,* Third Series, II (1901), 55-70.

_____ "Fundamental Beliefs of My Social Philosophy." *Forum,* XVIII (1894), 173-183.

_____ *Ground Under Our Feet: An Autobigraphy*. New York, 1938.

_____ "Industrial Liberty." American Economic Association, *Proceedings,* Third Series, III (1902), 59-79.

_____ "Municipal Ownership of Natural Monopolies." *North American Review,* CLXXII (1901), 445-455.

_____ "Progressivism True and False." *Review of Reviews.* LI (1915), 209-211.

_____ "Psychical Forces of Industry." *International Quarterly,* XI (1905), 301-315.

_____ *Socialism: An Examination of Its Nature, Strengths and Its Weaknesses, with Suggestions for Social Reform.* New York and Boston, 1894.

_____ *Social Law of Service.* New York, 1896.

_____ "Social Progress." *Cosmopolitan Magazine,* XXXI (1901), 61-64.

_____ "State Universities." *Cosmopolitan Magazine,* XIX (1895), 648-653.

_____ *Studies in the Evolution of Industrial Society.* New York, 1906.
"Keep the Universities Free!" *La Follette's Weekly Magazine,* July 2, 1910, pp. 3-4.

La Follette, Robert M. *La Follette's Autobiography.* Madison, 1960.

McCarthy, Charles. *The Wisconsin Idea.* New York, 1912.

Memorial Service in Honor of Charles Richard Van Hise. Madison, 1919.

Mood, Fulmer, ed. *The Early Writings of Frederick Jackson Turner.* Madison, 1938.

_____ ed. "Frederick Jackson Turner's Address on Education in a United States Without Free Lands." *Agricultural History,* XXIII (1949), 254-259.

Ross, Edward Alsworth. *Changing America: Studies in Contemporary Society.* New York, 1912.

_____ "Conscience of the Expert." *School and Society,* April 8, 1916, pp. 522-524.

_____ *Latter-day Saints and Sinners.* New York, 1910.

_____ "The Middle West: State Universities and Their Influence." *Century,* LXXXIII (1912), 874-880.

_____ "The Mob Mind." *Popular Science Monthly,* LI (1897), 390-398.

_____ *Seventy Years of It: An Autobiography.* New York, 1936.

_____ *Sin and Society: An Analysis of Latter-day Iniquity.* Boston and New York, 1907.

_____ *Social Control: A Survey of the Foundations of Order.* New York, 1918.

_____ "Training Citizens with 'Spunk' for Social Service." *Survey,* Aug. 29, 1914, p. 547.

State Board of Public Affairs. *Report Upon the Survey of the University of Wisconsin.* Madison, 1915.

Turner, Frederick Jackson. "The Democratic Education of the Middle West." *World's Work,* VI (1903), 3754-59.

_____ "The Extension Work of the University of Wisconsin." *University Extension,* I (1892) , 311-324.

_____ *The Frontier in American History.* New York, 1948.

_____ "Since the Foundation." Clark University Library, *Publications,* VII (1924) , no. 3, pp. 7-29.

_____ "Social Forces in American History." *American Historical Review,* XVI (1911) , 217-233.

Van Hise, Charles Richard. "Dangers Which Menace State Universities." *Journal of Education,* Aug. 11, 1910, pp. 90-91.

_____ "Educational Tendencies in State Universities." *Educational Review,* XXXIV (1907) , 504-520.

_____ "The Future of Man in America." *World's Work,* XVIII (1909) , 11718-24.

_____ "Inaugural Address," *Science,* New Series, Aug. 12, 1904, pp. 193-205.

_____ "Place of a University in a Democracy." *School and Society,* July 15, 1916, pp. 81-86.

_____ "The University and the State, Commencement Address at the University of Wisconsin, June 22, 1910." *La Follette's Weekly Magazine,* July 2, 1910, p. 7.

_____ "The Value of Scientific Training." *Colorado College Studies,* XI (1904) , 18-42.

B. Secondary and Interpretive Sources

Curti, Merle, and Vernon Carstensen. *The University of Wisconsin: A History* 1848-1925. 2 vols. Madison, 1949.

Dorfman, Joseph. *The Economic Mind in American Civilization.* Vol. III. New York, 1949.

Everett, John Rutherford. *Religion in Economics, A Study of John Bates Clark, Richard T. Ely, Simon N. Patten.* New York, 1946.

Fine, Sydney. "Richard T. Ely, Forerunner of Progressivism, 1880-1901." *Mississippi Valley Historical Review,* XXXVI (1951) , 599-624.

Fitzpatrick, Edward A. *McCarthy of Wisconsin.* New York, 1944.

Harter, La Fayette George, Jr. *John R. Commons: His Assault on Laissez-faire.* Corvallis, 1962.

Holmes, Fred L. *Regulation of Railroads and Public Utilities in Wisconsin.* New York, 1915.

Howe, Frederick C. *Wisconsin: An Experiment in Democracy.* New York, 1912.

John R. Commons: Addresses Delivered on October Tenth, 1950 *in Commemoration of His Achievements as a Teacher, Economist, and Administrator.* Madison, 1952.

La Follette, Belle Case and Fola. *Robert M. La Follette.* 2 vols. New York, 1953.

McMurray, Howard J. "Some Influences of the University of Wisconsin on the State Government of Wisconsin." Unpublished doctoral dissertation, University of Wisconsin, 1940.

Maxwell, Robert S. *La Follette and the Rise of the Progressives in Wisconsin.* Madison, 1956.

Slosson, E. E. *Great American Universities.* New York, 1910.

Steffens, Lincoln. *The Autobiography of Lincoln Steffens.* New York and Chicago, 1937.

———— "The Mind of a State." *La Follette's Weekly Magazine,* Jan. 9, 1909, pp. 5, 13.

Vance, Maurice. *Charles Richard Van Hise, Scientist Progressive.* Madison, 1960.

III. IRVING BABBITT

A Selected Works by Babbitt

"Are the English Critical?" *Nation,* March 21 and 28, 1912, pp. 282-284, 309-311.

"Bergson and Rousseau." *Nation,* Nov. 14, 1912, pp. 452-455.

"The Breakdown of Internationalism." *Nation,* June 17 and 24, 1915, pp. 677-680, 704-706.

"Culture and Scholarship." *Nation,* July 2, 1908, pp. 7-8.

Democracy and Leadership. Boston and New York, 1924.

The Dhammapada: Translated from the Pali with an Essay on Buddha and the Occident. New York, 1936. Translated by Babbitt.

"Experience and Dogma." *Saturday Review of Literature,* Nov. 1, 1930, pp. 287-299.

"Ferdinand Brunetiere." *Atlantic Monthly,* XCIX (1907), 530-536.

"Ferdinand Brunetiere and His Critical Method." *Atlantic Monthly,* LXXIX (1897), 757-766.

"Genius and Taste." *Nation,* Feb. 7, 1918, pp. 138-141.

Humanist and Specialist. Providence, 1926.

"Humanistic Education in China and the West." *Chinese Students' Monthly,* XVII (1921), 85-91.

"Humanists and Humanitarians." *Nation,* Sept. 2, 1915, pp. 288-289.

Literature and the American College: Essays in Defense of the Humanities. Chicago, 1956.

The Masters of Modern French Criticism. Boston and New York, 1912.

"Modern Stoicism." *Forum,* LXXXII (1929), x, xii, xiv.

The New Laokoon. Boston, 1910.

On Being Creative. Boston and New York, 1932.

Rousseau and Romanticism. New York, 1960.

"Schiller and Romanticism." *Modern Language Notes,* XXXVII (1922), 257-268.

"Sociology and Humanism." *Nation,* June 8, 1916, p. 620.

Spanish Character and Other Essays. Boston and New York, 1940.

B. Selected Works Relating to Babbitt

Adams, James Luther. "Humanism and Creation." *Hound and Horn,* VI (1932), 173-196.

Calverton, V. F. "Humanism: Literary Fascism." *New Masses,* V (1930), 9-10.

Cappon, Alexander P. "Irving Babbitt and His Fundamental Thinking." *New Humanist,* VI (1933), 9-13.

"Chronicle and Comment." *Bookman,* LXXI (1930), 65-80.

Collins, Seward. "Criticism in America." *Bookman,* LXXI (1930), 241-256, 353-364, 400-415; LXXII (1930), 145-164, 209-228.

Eliot, T. S. "The Humanism of Irving Babbitt." *Forum,* LXXX (1928), 37-44.

Elliott, G. R. "The Religious Dissension of Babbitt and More." *American Review,* IX (1937), 252-265.

———— "Irving Babbitt as I Knew Him." *American Review,* VIII (1936), 36-60.

Foerster, Norman, ed. *Humanism and America.* New York, 1930.

Giese, W. F. "Irving Babbitt, Undergraduate." *American Review,* VI (1935), 65-94.

Grabo, Carl H. "The Case of Mr. Babbitt." *New Humanist,* VI (1933), 29-34.

Grattan, C. Hartley, ed. *The Critique of Humanism.* New York, 1930.

Grosselin, Dom Oliver. *The Intuitive Voluntarism of Irving Babbitt.* Latrobe, Pa., 1951.

Hecht, Hans. Review of Irving Babbitt, *Rousseau and Romanticism,* in *Englische Studien,* LV (1921), 447-457.

Hough, Lynn Harold. *Great Humanists.* New York, 1952.

Jones, Howard Mumford. "Professor Babbitt Cross-Examined." *New Republic,* March 21, 1928, pp. 158-160.

Kariel, Henry S. "The Political Conservatism of Irving Babbitt." Unpublished master's thesis, Stanford University, 1950.

Kirk, Russell. "The Conservative Humanism of Irving Babbitt." *Prairie Schooner,* XXVI (1952), 245-255.

———— *The Conservative Mind.* Chicago, 1960.

Leander, Folke. "Humanism and Naturalism," in *Goteborgs Hogskolas Arsskrift*, XLIII (1937), 1-227.

Levin, Harry. *Irving Babbitt and the Teaching of Literature.* n.p., 1960.

Lippmann, Walter. "Humanism as Dogma." *Saturday Review of Literature*, March 15, 1930, pp. 817-819.

McKean, Keith F. *The Moral Measure of Literature.* Denver, 1961.

McMahon, Francis E. *The Humanism of Irving Babbitt.* Washington, 1931.

Manchester, Frederick, and Odell Shepard, eds. *Irving Babbitt: Man and Teacher.* New York, 1941.

Mather, Frank Jewett. "Irving Babbitt." *Harvard Graduates' Magazine*, XLII (1933), 65-84.

Mencken, H. L. "The State of the Country." *American Mercury*, III (1924), 123-125.

Mercier, Louis J. A. *American Humanism and the New Age.* Milwaukee, 1948.

—————— "Was Irving Babbitt a Naturalist?" *New Scholasticism, XXVII* (1953), 39-71.

More, Paul Elmer. "Irving Babbitt." *University of Toronto Quarterly*, III (1933-34), 129-145.

Munson, Gorham. *The Dilemma of the Liberated.* New York, 1930.

Nickerson, Hoffman. "Irving Babbitt." *American Review*, II (1934), 385-404.

Pritchard, John Paul. *Return to the Fountains.* Durham, 1942.

Wilbur, Russell. "A Word About Babbitt." *Commonweal*, Jan. 25, 1935, pp. 364-366.

Wilson, Edmund. "Notes on Babbitt and More." *New Republic*, March 19, 1930, pp. 115-120.

IV. ALBERT JAY NOCK

A. Frequent Articles and Regular Columns by Nock

American Magazine, 1910-1914. New York.

American Mercury, 1924-1940. New York.

Freeman, 1920-1924. New York.

Scribner's Commentator, 1940-1942.

B. Other Selected Articles and Books by Nock

Letters from Albert Jay Nock, 1924-1945, to Edmund C. Evans, Mrs. Edmund C. Evans, and Ellen Winsor. Caldwell, Idaho, 1949.

"The Absurdity of Teaching English." *Bookman*, LXIX (1929), 113-119.

"Alas, Poor Yorick!" *Harper's*, CLIX (1929), 56-62.

"Artemus Ward." *Saturday Review of Literature*, Oct. 4, 1924, pp. 157-158.

The Book of Journeyman. New York, 1930.

"The Bright Isle." *Atlantic Monthly,* CLIX (1937) , 552-559.

"The Decline of Conversation." *Harper's,* CLII (1926) , 696-702.

"Epstean's Law." *Atlantic Monthly,* CLXVI (1940) , 430-435.

Free Speech and Plain Language. New York, 1937.

Henry George. New York, 1939.

"In Defense of the Individual." *Atlantic Monthly,* CLXV (1940) , 833-839.

Jefferson. New York, 1926.

Journal of Forgotten Days, May 1934-*October* 1935. Hinsdale, Illinois, 1948.

"Life, Liberty, and . . . " *Scribner's Magazine,* XCVII (1935) , 150-154.

"Lincoln Steffens." *Saturday Review of Literature,* May 9, 1931, pp. 809-810.

"A Little Conserva-tive." *Atlantic Monthly,* CLVIII (1936) , 481-489.

Memoirs of a Superfluous Man. New York, 1943.

"Officialism and Lawlessness." *Harper's,* CLX (1929) , 11-19.

On Doing the Right Thing and Other Essays. New York, 1928.

"On the Practice of Smoking in Church." *Harper's,* CLX (1930) , 314-321.

Our Enemy, the State. New York, 1935.

"Peace the Aristocrat." *Atlantic Monthly,* CXV (1915) , 539-599.

The Theory of Education in the United States. New York, 1932.

"Utopia in Pennsylvania: The Amish." *Atlantic Monthly,* CLXVII (1941) , 478-484.

"The Value to the Clergyman of Training in the Classics." *School Review,* XVI (1908) , 383-390.

"What Are Elections For?" *Virginia Quarterly Review,* IX (1933) , 1-13.

C. Selected Works Relating to Nock

Crunden, Robert M. *The Mind and Art of Albert Jay Nock.* Chicago, 1964.

Dewey, John. "Bending the Twig." *New Republic,* April 13, 1932, pp. 242-244.

Flexner, Abraham. "Education in America." *Nation,* Feb. 17, 1932, pp. 207-208.

Nevins, Allan, ed. *The Letters and Journal of Brand Whitlock.* 2 vols. New York, 1936.

Nock, Francis J., ed. *Selected Letters of Albert Jay Nock with Memories of Albert Jay Nock by Ruth Robinson.* Caldwell, Idaho, 1962.

Turner, Susan J. *A History of the Freeman.* New York, 1963.

V. ABRAHAM FLEXNER

A. Selected Works by Flexner

Abraham Flexner: An Autobiography. New York, 1960.

"Address." American Philosophical Society, *Proceedings,* LXIX (1930), 257-269.

"Adjusting the College to American Life." *Science,* March 5, 1909, pp. 361-372.

The American College. New York, 1908.

"Aristocratic and Democratic Education." *Atlantic Monthly,* CVIII (1911), 386-395.

The Burden of Humanism. Oxford, England, 1928.

"College Entrance Examinations." *Popular Science Monthly,* LXIII (1903), 53-60.

Daniel Coit Gilman. New York, 1946.

Do Americans Really Value Education? Cambridge, 1927.

"Education as Mental Discipline." *Atlantic Monthly,* CXIX (1917), 452-464.

"Failings of Our Graduate Schools." *Atlantic Monthly,* CXLIX (1932), 441-452.

Funds and Foundations. New York, 1952.

Henry S. Pritchett. New York, 1943.

I Remember: the Autobiography of Abraham Flexner. New York, 1940.

"Is Social Work a Profession?" *School and Society,* June 26, 1915, pp. 901-911.

"Medical Colleges." *World's Work,* XXI (1911), 14238-14242.

Medical Education: A Comparative Study. New York, 1925.

Medical Education in Europe. Bulletin Number Six of the Carnegie Foundation for the Advancement of Teaching. New York, 1912.

Medical Education in the United States and Canada. Bulletin Number Four of the Carnegie Foundation for the Advancement of Teaching. New York, 1910.

A Modern College and a Modern School. New York, 1923.

"A Modern University." *Atlantic Monthly,* CXXXVI (1925), 530-541.

"Parents and Schools." *Atlantic Monthly,* CXVIII (1916), 25-33.

"The Plethora of Doctors." *Atlantic Monthly,* CVI (1910), 20-25.

"The Preparatory School." *Atlantic Monthly,* XCIV (1904), 368-377.

"The Prepared Mind." *School and Society,* June 26, 1937, pp. 865-872.

"Private Fortunes and the Public Future." *Atlantic Monthly,* CLVI (1935), 215-224.

"The Problem of College Pedagogy." *Atlantic Monthly,* CIII (1909), 838-844.

Prostitution in Europe. New York, 1914.

"Purpose in the American College." *School and Society,* Dec. 12, 1925, pp. 729-736.

"Remarks of the Director at the Organization Meeting." Institute for Advanced Study, *Bulletin,* Number One, Dec. 1930, pp. 7-14.

Universities: American, English, German. New York, 1930.

"The University in American Life." *Atlantic Monthly,* CXLIX (1932), 620-627.

"Upbuilding American Education." *Independent,* Aug. 9, 1915, pp. 188-191.

"The Usefulness of Useless Knowledge. *Harper's,* CLXXIX (1939), 544-552.

B. Selected Works Relating to Flexner

Bode, B. H. "Currents and Cross Currents in Higher Education." *Journal of Higher Education,* II (1931), 374-379.

Coffman, L. D. "Flexner and the State University." _Journal of Higher Education,* II (1931), 380-383.

Cowley, W. H. "The University and the Individual." *Journal of Higher Education,* II (1931), 390-396.

Kilpatrick, William H. "Universities: American, English, and German." *Journal of Higher Education,* II (1931), 357-363.

MacCracken, Henry N. "Flexner and the Woman's College." *Journal of Higher Education,* II (1931), 367-373.

VI.   ROBERT MAYNARD HUTCHINS

A.   Frequent Articles by Hutchins

School and Society, 1932-1962.   New York.

University of Chicago Magazine, 1930-1952.   Chicago.

B.   Other Selected Articles and Books by Hutchins

"Address." American Law Institute, *Proceedings,* VI (1928), 592-601.

"The American Educational System." *School Record,* XLI (1933), 95-100.

"The Atomic Bomb versus Civilization." *Journal of the NEA,* XXXV (1946), 114-117.

"Blueprint for Wartime Education." *Saturday Evening Post,* Aug. 15, 1942, pp. 17, 69-72.

"The Challenge of the Market Place." *Nation's Business,* XXIX (1941), 24-26, 49.

"The College and the Needs of Society." *Journal of General Education,* III (1949), 175-181.

"The Colleges and Public Service." *Bulletin of the Association of American Colleges,* XXIV (1938), 31-35.

"The Coming Boom in Education." *Vital Speeches,* Dec. 2, 1935, pp. 136-137.

The Conflict in Education in a Democratic Society. New York, 1953.

"Connecticut and the Yale Law School." *Connecticut Bar Journal,* II (1928), 1-9.

"The Constitutional Foundations for World Order," in *Foundations for World Order.* Denver, 1949.

"Dark Hours in Our History." *Vital Speeches,* July 1, 1941, pp. 569-570.

"Democracy and Education." *Vital Speeches,* July 15, 1939, pp. 586-588.

"Dissenting Opinion as a Creative Art." *Saturday Review,* Aug. 12, 1961, pp. 12, 35-36.

"Do We Want Permanent Conscription? No." *Colliers,* June 9, 1945, pp. 15, 27.

"Education and Social Improvement." *Vital Speeches,* June 1, 1938. pp. 498-501.

"Education and the Duration." *Christian Century,* Feb. 10, 1943, pp. 162-164.

Education for Freedom. Baton Rouge, 1943.

"Education for Freedom." *Christian Century,* Nov. 15, 1944, pp. 1314-1316.

"Education for Freedom." *Harper's,* CLXXXIII (1941), 512-526.

"Education in the Army." *Christian Century,* Dec. 19, 1951, pp. 1474-1475.

Freedom, Education, and the Fund. New York, 1956.

"The Freedom of the University." *Ethics,* LXI (1951), 95-104.

"The Future of the Wall." *America,* Jan. 26, 1963, pp. 146-148.

"Gate Receipts and Glory." *Saturday Evening Post,* Dec. 3, 1938, pp. 23, 73-77.

"Grammar, Rhetoric, and Mr. Dewey." *Social Frontier,* III (1937), 137-139.

The Great Conversation: The Substance of a Liberal Education. Chicago, 1952.

"Hard Times and the Higher Learning." *Yale Review,* n.s. XXII (1933), 714-730.

"The High Cost of Prejudice." *Phylon,* XII (1951), 101-105.

"The Higher Learning: 1940." *Commonweal,* May 31, 1940, pp. 112-114.

"The Higher Learning in America." *Journal of Higher Education,* IV (1933), 1-8.

The Higher Learning in America. New Haven, 1936.

"Hutchins Answers Hutchins." *Saturday Evening Post,* Sept. 24, 1938, pp. 23, 34, 36.

"The Idea of a College." *Measure,* I (1950), 361-371.

"Ideals in Education." *American Journal of Sociology*, XLIII (1937), 1-15.

"An Institute of Human Relations." *American Journal of Sociology*, XXXV (1929), 187-193.

"Is Democracy Possible?" *Saturday Review*, Feb. 21, 1959, pp. 15-17, 58.

"The Issue in the Higher Learning." *International Journal of Ethics*, XLIV (1934), 175-184.

"The Law and the Psychologists." *Yale Review*, n.s. XVI (1927), 678-690.

"The Law School Tomorrow." *North American Review*, CCXXV (1928), 129-140.

"Learning to Live." *Ladies Home Journal*, LXIII (1946), 24-25, 209.

"Legal Education." *Vital Speeches*, March 1, 1937, pp. 306-310.

"Let's Split the Educational Atom." *Colliers*, Dec. 7, 1946, pp. 80, 87.

"The Meaning and Significance of Academic Freedom." *Annals of the American Academy of Political and Social Science*, CCC (1955), 72-78.

"A Message to the Young Generation." *Common Cause*, IV (1951), 393-397.

Morals, Religion and Higher Education. Chicago, 1950.

"A New Plan for Higher Education." *Review of Reviews*, LXXXVII (1933), 35, 53.

"The New Realism." *Commonweal*, July 5, 1945, pp. 282-284.

"The Newer Orthodoxy." *New Republic*, Feb. 7, 1955, pp. 14-16.

"The Next Fifty Years." *Science*, XCIV (1941), 333-335.

No Friendly Voice. Chicago, 1936.

"On Democracy and Defense." *Common Ground*, I (1940), 57-61.

"On Service and Self." *Rotarian*, LXVI (1945), 8-9.

"Opportunities in Library Service." *Journal of the NEA*, XXVI (1937), 138.

The Political Animal. Santa Barbara, 1962.

"A Reply to Professor Whitehead." *Atlantic Monthly*, CLVIII (1936), 582-588.

"Review of *Mission of the University* by Jose Ortega y Gasset." *Annals of the American Academy of Political and Social Science*, CCXXXIX (1945), 217-220.

St. Thomas and the World State. Milwaukee, 1949.

"Schools Must Prove Right to be Supported." *Rotarian*, LXI (1942), 14, 56-57.

Some Observations on American Education. Cambridge, England, 1956.

Some Questions About Education in North America. Toronto, 1952.

The State of the University, 1929-1949. Chicago, 1949.

"The Theory of the State: Edmund Burke." *Review of Politics*, V (1943), 139-155.

"The Threat to American Education." *Colliers*, Dec. 30, 1944. pp. 20-21.

"Toward a Durable Society." *Fortune*, XXVII (1943), 158-160, 194-207.

"Tradition in Education." *Vital Speeches*, Feb. 15, 1938, pp. 258-262.

"Train Minds to Meet Problems." *Rotarian*, LXIX (1946), 14, 62-63.

"Training Professors—and Paying Them." *Review of Reviews*, LXXXI (1930), 99-100.

"T. S. Eliot on Education." *Measure*, I (1950), 1-8.

Two Faces of Federalism. Santa Barbara, 1961.

"Uncle Sam's Children." *Saturday Evening Post*, Jan. 28, 1939, pp. 23, 76-79.

"The University and Character." *Commonweal*, April 22, 1938, pp. 710-711.

"The University and the Mind of the Age." *Measure*, I (1950), 133-141.

"University Education." *Yale Review*, n.s. XXV (1936), 665-682.

The University of Utopia. Chicago, 1953.

"The University of Utopia." *Yale Review*, n.s. XX (1931), 456-486.

"The Value of the Museum." *Science*, Oct. 15, 1943, pp. 331-334.

"Victory Must Begin at Home!" *Christian Century*, April 29, 1942, pp. 554-556.

"We Are Getting No Brighter." *Saturday Evening Post*, Dec. 11, 1937, pp. 5-7, 98.

"What Can We Do About It?" *Saturday Evening Post*, Feb. 19, 1938, pp. 27-28, 73-75.

"What Every Schoolgirl Ought to Know." *Women's Home Companion*, LXIX (1942), 13, 42-43.

"What Good Are Endowments?" *Saturday Evening Post*, Nov. 11, 1939, pp. 8-9, 40-46.

"What Is a University?" *Vital Speeches*, May 20, 1935, pp. 547-549.

"What Is the Job of Our Colleges?" *New York Times Magazine*, March 7, 1937, pp. 1-2.

"Where Do We Go From Here in Education?" *Vital Speeches*, July 15, 1947, pp. 591-594.

"Why Go to College?" *Saturday Evening Post*, Jan. 22, 1938, pp. 16-17, 72, 74.

"Why Send Them to School?" *Saturday Evening Post*, Dec. 25, 1937, pp. 10-11, 30-31.

"The Yale Law School in 1928." *Connecticut Bar Journal*, II (1928), 1-9.

C. Selected Works Relating to Hutchins

Adler, Mortimer J. "The Chicago School." *Harper's*, CLXXXIII (1941), 377-388.

———— "God and the Professors," in *Science, Philosophy, and Religion, a Symposium.* New York, 1941.

Arnstein, George Ernest. "The Great Books Program and its Educational Philosophy." Unpublished doctoral dissertation, University of California, 1953.

Buchanan, Scott. "The Metaphysics of the Higher Learning." *Southern Review*, IV (1938) , 1-14.

Chase, Harry Woodburn. "Hutchins' 'Higher Learning' Grounded." *American Scholar*, VI (1937) , 236-244.

Clark, Charles E. "The Higher Learning in a Democracy." *International Journal of Ethics*, XLVII (1937) , 317-335.

Cohen, Arthur A., ed. *Humanistic Education and Western Civilization: Essays for Robert M. Hutchins.* New York, 1964.

Dewey, John. " 'The Higher Learning in America.' " *Social Frontier*, III (1937) , 167-169.

_____ "President Hutchins' Proposals To Remake Higher Education." *Social Frontier*, III (1937) , 103-104.

Faculty of the College of the University of Chicago. *The Idea and Practice of General Education.* Chicago, 1950.

Foerster, Norman. "Chicago and General Education." *American Review*, V (1935) , 404-419.

Frodin, Reuben. "Bibliography of Robert M. Hutchins, 1925-1950." *Journal of General Education*, IV (1950) , 303-324.

Gallagher, Buell G. "Mr. Hutchins and Mr. Dewey." *Christian Century*, Jan. 24, 1945, pp. 106-107.

Gideonse, Harry D. *The Higher Learning in a Democracy.* New York, 1937.

Hook, Sidney. "Six Fallacies of Robert Hutchins." *New Leader*, March 19, 1956, pp. 18-28.

Kimpton, Lawrence A. *The State of the University.* [Chicago] 1953.

MacDonald, Dwight. "The Book-of-the-Millennium Club." *New Yorker*, Nov. 29, 1952, pp. 171-188.

Mayer, Milton S. "Hutchins of Chicago." *Harper's* CLXXVIII (1939) , 344-355, 543-552.

Schwinn, Bonaventure. "Hutchins, Cowley, and Pope Pius XI." *Catholic World*, CLIV (1941) , 22-29.

Smith, T. V. "The Chicago School." *International Journal of Ethics*, XLVI (1936) , 378-387.

Taylor, Harold. "A Conservative Educator." *New Republic*, March 22, 1954, pp. 16-17.

Weber, Pearl L. "Universities and First Principles." *Education*, LX (1939) , 42-47.

Wecter, Dixon. "Can Metaphysics Save the World?" *Saturday Review*, April 10, 1948, pp. 7, 8, 30-32.

Zunzer, Robert F. "Robert Maynard Hutchins' Conceptions of the Functions and Structures of Higher Education." Unpublished doctoral dissertation, Stanford University, 1951.

VII. ALEXANDER MEIKLEJOHN

A. Selected Works by Meiklejohn

Amherst Graduates' Quarterly, 1911-1925. Amherst.

"Adult Education: A Fresh Start." *New Republic*, Aug. 15, 1934, pp. 14-17.

"The Aim of the Liberal College," in Maurice G. Fulton, ed., *College Life*. New York, 1921.

"The American College and American Freedom." *Congressional Record*, pp. 8751-8755, 85th Congress. Washington, 1957.

"The College and the Common Life." *Harper's*, CXLVII (1923), 721-726.

"College Education and the Moral Ideal." *Education*, XXVIII (1908), 552-567.

"The Colleges and the S.A.T.C." *Nation*, Dec. 7, 1918, pp. 697-698.

"Congress and the People." *Nation*, Nov 7, 1942, pp. 369-371.

"Democracy Held Success, Not Popular Delusion." *New York Times*, Dec. 17, 1922, Section 8, p. 2.

"The Devil's Revenge: For What Is the Scholar Responsible?" *Century*, CVII (1924), 718-723.

"Education as a Factor in Post-War Reconstruction." *Free World*, V (1943), 27-31.

Education Between Two Worlds. New York, 1942.

"Education Under the Charter." *Free World*, X (1945), 37-39.

"Educational Cooperation Between Church and State." *Law and Contemporary Problems*, XIV (1949), 61-72.

"Educational Leadership in America." *Harper's*, CLX (1930), 440-447.

"Everything Worth Saying Should Be Said." *New York Times Magazine*, July 18, 1948, pp. 8, 32.

"The Evils of College Athletics." *Harper's Weekly*, Dec. 2, 1905, pp. 1751-1752.

The Experimental College. New York, 1932.

"Fiat Justitia—The College as Critic." *Harvard Graduates' Magazine*, XXVI (1917), 1-14.

"The First Amendment and Evils That Congress Has a Right to Prevent." *Indiana Law Journal*, XXVI (1951), 447-493.

"For International Citizenship." *Adult Education Journal*, II (1943), 44-47.

Free Speech and Its Relation to Self-Government. New York, 1948.

Freedom and the College. New York, 1923.

"Freedom and the People." *Nation*, Dec. 12, 1953, pp. 500-503.

"Freedom of the College." *Atlantic Monthly,* CXXI (1918), 83-89.

"From Church to State," in Willard L. Sperry, ed., *Religion and Education.* Cambridge, 1945.

"The Future of Liberal Education." *New Republic,* Jan. 25, 1943, pp. 113-115.

"Higher Education in a Democracy." *North Central Association Quarterly,* XVI (1941), 149-154.

"In Memoriam: An Address Delivered in Boston on the Anniversary of the Execution of Sacco and Vanzetti." *New Republic,* Sept. 5, 1928, pp. 69-71.

"Integrity of the Universities—How to Defend It." *Bulletin of the Atomic Scientists,* IX (1953), 193-194.

"Intercollegiate Athletics." *Outlook,* March 8, 1922, p. 387.

"Is Mental Training a Myth?" *Educational Review,* XXXVII (1909), 126-141.

"Is Our World Christian?" in *Some Addresses Delivered at Amherst College, Commencement Time,* June, 1923. [Amherst] 1924.

The Liberal College. Boston, 1920.

"A Liberal Education." *The Kindergarten-Primary Magazine,* XXVII (1914), 2.

"Liberty—For What?" *Harper's,* CLXXI (1935), 364-372.

"Mr. Hutchins' Dogma." *New Republic,* Aug. 2, 1943, pp. 147-148.

"A New College." *Century,* CIX (1925), 312-320.

"A New College." *New Republic,* April 14, 1926, pp. 215-218.

"A New College with a New Idea." *New York Times Magazine,* May 29, 1927, pp. 1, 2, 21.

"Pharisees and Reformers." *Nation,* July 4, 1923, p. 13.

"Philosophers and Others." *Philosophical Review,* XXXIV (1925), 262-280.

Philosophy. Chicago, 1926.

"The Place of Student Activities." *Education,* XXXV (1915), 312-319.

Political Freedom: The Constitutional Powers of the People. New York, 1960.

"President Meiklejohn's Farewell Address." *School and Society,* July 7, 1923, pp. 12-16.

"The Priority of the Market Place of Ideas," in Law School of the University of Chicago, *Conference on Freedom and the Law,* Conference Series, No. 13, May 7, 1953, pp. 3-15.

"The Purpose of the Liberal College." *NEA Journal of Proceedings and Addresses of the Fifty-second Annual Meeting,* 102-103. Saint Paul, 1914.

"Rejoinder." *Nation,* March 25, 1931, pp. 325-326.

"A Reply to John Dewey." *Fortune,* XXXI (1945), 207-219.

"Report of the Commission on the Organization of the College Curriculum." Association of American Colleges, *Bulletin,* IX (1923) , 79-90.

"Required Education for Freedom." *American Scholar,* XIII (1944) , 393-395.

"A Schoolmaster's View of Compulsory Military Training." Academy of Political Science, *Proceedings,* VI (1916) , 595-602.

"Sedition Circa 400 B.C." *Nation,* April 23, 1955, pp. 349-352.

"Should Communists Be Allowed to Teach?" *New York Times Magazine,* March 27, 1949, pp. 10, 64-66.

"Teachers and Controversial Questions." *Harper's,* CLXXVII (1938) , 15-22.

"The Teaching of Intellectual Freedom." *Bulletin of the AAUP,* XXXVIII (1952) , 10-25.

"To Teach the World How to Be Free." *New York Times Magazine,* Aug. 11, 1946, pp. 5, 48-50.

"To Whom Are We Responsible?" *Century,* CVI (1923) , 643-650.

"The Unity of the Curriculum." *New Republic,* supplement, Oct. 25, 1922, pp. 2-3.

"The Values of Logic and the College Curriculum." *Religious Education,* VII (1912) , 62-68.

"What Are College Games For?" *Atlantic Monthly,* CXXX (1922) , 663-671.

"What Constitutes Preparation for College: The College View." *Education,* XXXI (1911) , 578-584.

What Does America Mean? New York, 1935.

"What Does the First Amendment Mean?" *University of Chicago Law Review,* XX (1953) , 461-479.

"What Next in Progressive Education." *Progressive Education,* VI (1929) , 99-110.

"Who Should Go to College?" *New Republic,* Jan. 16, 1929, pp. 238-241.

"Wisconsin's Experimental College." *Survey,* June 1, 1927, pp. 268-270, 294-295.

"Woodrow Wilson, Teacher." *Saturday Review of Literature,* May 30, 1925, pp. 785-786.

B. Selected Works Relating to Meiklejohn

Abbott, Lawrence F. "A New College and an Old One." *Outlook,* Sept. 24, 1924, pp. 116-117.

Barr, Stringfellow. "Education and Unfinished Business." *Free World,* V (1943) , 184.

Dewey, John. "Dewey vs. Meiklejohn." *Fortune,* XXXI (1945) , 10, 14.

————— "The Meiklejohn Experiment." *New Republic,* Aug. 17, 1932, pp. 23-24.

Erskine, John. *My Life as a Teacher.* Philadelphia and New York, 1948.

Fuess, Claude Moore. *Amherst: The Story of a New England College.* Boston, 1935.

Gaus, John Merriman. "The Issues at Amherst." *Nation,* July 4, 1923, p. 12.

Greene, Bancroft. "The Educational Philosophy of Alexander Meiklejohn." Unpublished senior thesis, Amherst College, 1964.

Heilman, Robert B. "Light on a Darkling Plain." *Sewanee Review,* LII (1944), 176-190.

Hill, Walker H. *Learning and Living: Proceedings of an Anniversary Celebration in Honor of Alexander Meiklejohn.* Chicago, 1942.

Lovett, Robert Morss. "Meiklejohn of Amherst." *New Republic,* July 4, 1923, pp. 146-148.

"A Misplaced Man." *Freeman,* July 4, 1923, pp. 388-389.

Powell, John W. *Education for Maturity.* New York, 1949.

———— *School for Americans.* New York, 1942.

Price, Lucien. "Americans We Like: Alexander Meiklejohn." *Nation,* Nov. 16, 1927, pp. 541-542.

———— *Prophets Unawares.* New York, 1924.

"Resignation of President Meiklejohn at Amherst." *School and Society,* June 30, 1923, pp. 714-715.

Taylor, Harold. "Meiklejohn: The Art of Making People Think." *New York Times Magazine,* May 5, 1957, pp. 20, 22.

Vivas, Eliseo. "Wisconsin's Experimental College." *Nation,* March 25, 1931, pp. 322-325.

INDEX